★ ★ ★ ★ ★

**STUDIES
IN
DEFENSE
POLICY**

★ ★ ★ ★ ★

U.S. Tactical Air Power

Missions, Forces, and Costs

WILLIAM D. WHITE

THE BROOKINGS INSTITUTION

U.S. TACTICAL AIR POWER

Studies in Defense Policy
TITLES PUBLISHED

WILLIAM D. WHITE

U.S. TACTICAL AIR POWER
Missions, Forces, and Costs

THE BROOKINGS INSTITUTION
Washington, D.C.

Copyright © 1974 by
THE BROOKINGS INSTITUTION
1775 Massachusetts Avenue, N.W., Washington, D.C. 20036

Library of Congress Cataloging in Publication Data:
White, William D   1939–
  U.S. tactical air power.
  (Studies in defense policy)
  Includes bibliographical references.
  1. Aeronautics, Military—United States.   2. United
States. Air Force—Weapons systems.   3. United States.
Air Force—Procurement.   4. Air power.   I. Title.
II. Series.
UG633.W397   358.4′00973   74-20695
ISBN 0-8157-9371-5

9 8 7 6 5 4 3 2 1

THE BROOKINGS INSTITUTION is an independent organization devoted to nonpartisan research, education, and publication in economics, government, foreign policy, and the social sciences generally. Its principal purposes are to aid in the development of sound public policies and to promote public understanding of issues of national importance.

The Institution was founded on December 8, 1927, to merge the activities of the Institute for Government Research, founded in 1916, the Institute of Economics, founded in 1922, and the Robert Brookings Graduate School of Economics and Government, founded in 1924.

The Board of Trustees is responsible for the general administration of the Institution, while the immediate direction of the policies, program, and staff is vested in the President, assisted by an advisory committee of the officers and staff. The by-laws of the Institution state, "It is the function of the Trustees to make possible the conduct of scientific research, and publication, under the most favorable conditions, and to safeguard the independence of the research staff in the pursuit of their studies and in the publication of the results of such studies. It is not a part of their function to determine, control, or influence the conduct of particular investigations or the conclusions reached."

The President bears final responsibility for the decision to publish a manuscript as a Brookings book or staff paper. In reaching his judgment on the competence, accuracy, and objectivity of each study, the President is advised by the director of the appropriate research program and weighs the views of a panel of expert outside readers who report to him in confidence on the quality of the work. Publication of a work signifies that it is deemed to be a competent treatment worthy of public consideration; such publication does not imply endorsement of conclusions or recommendations contained in the study.

The Institution maintains its position of neutrality on issues of public policy in order to safeguard the intellectual freedom of the staff. Hence interpretations or conclusions in Brookings publications should be understood to be solely those of the author or authors and should not be attributed to the Institution, to its trustees, officers, or other staff members, or to the organizations that support its research.

FOREWORD

In less than four decades, the importance of air power within U.S. conventional military forces has risen dramatically, from the minor support role assigned it before World War II to its present status, in which it claims a share of the defense budget equal to that of the combined land forces of the Army and the Marine Corps. Over $5 billion more will be spent on U.S. tactical air forces in fiscal year 1975 than on all the components of the strategic nuclear forces, offensive and defensive. Yet because of the continuing sharp increase in aircraft costs, the tactical air forces are receiving fewer aircraft and modernizing more slowly than at any time since the emphasis on U.S. conventional capabilities was renewed at the beginning of the 1960s.

Faced with an aging and dwindling aircraft inventory, the tactical air forces must soon choose between accepting still higher levels of spending for tactical air power and making major adjustments in either their strength or their composition. This paper sets forth the reasons underlying the rise of U.S. tactical air power; describes existing forces and the major programs under way for acquiring new weapon systems; and documents the upward trend in aircraft costs and the reasons for it. The author suggests four alternatives to the present course, provides illustrative force structures for each, and weighs the budgets and effects on existing mission capability that would evolve.

William D. White carried out the study while a research associate on the defense analysis staff of the Brookings Foreign Policy Studies program.

The Brookings Institution is grateful to the members of its Defense Analysis Advisory Board who reviewed the paper—George H. Quester, Stanley R. Resor, General Matthew B. Ridgway, and Charles Rossotti. The author wishes to thank John F. Ahearne, Phil E. DePoy, George H. Haering, Lieutenant General Glenn A. Kent, K. P. Rice, and the staffs of Major General Leslie W. Bray, Jr., and Colonel W. G. Skelton for their constructive comments on earlier drafts. The suggestions and assistance of the author's colleagues at Brookings—Major Thomas I. Anderson, Commander Ted Baker, Edward R. Fried, Jeffrey Record, and Alton H. Quanbeck—are also gratefully acknowledged. Elizabeth H. Cross edited the manuscript; Gail L. Zirkel typed it.

The Institution acknowledges the assistance of the Ford Foundation for its supporting grant to defense studies. The views expressed are those of the author and should not be attributed to the Ford Foundation or the trustees, officers, or other staff of the Brookings Institution.

KERMIT GORDON
President

August 1974
Washington, D.C.

CONTENTS

Tables

Figures

CHAPTER ONE

INTRODUCTION

No other nation counts so heavily on air power for its conventional military strength or spends so much on its tactical air forces as does the United States. By conservative estimate the direct costs of operating, maintaining, and modernizing baseline U.S. tactical air forces will amount to more than $17 billion in fiscal 1975. Including an apportioned share of nonmission support costs and general military overhead, tactical air power will consume fully one-fourth of the 1975 defense budget. Through 1980, under the present course, direct spending on U.S. tactical air forces is projected to exceed $100 billion (in dollars of constant fiscal year 1975 purchasing power), and indirect costs imputed to these elements of the mission forces will add another $40 billion or more.

The American public has not only the right but the responsibility to ask if these dollars are being wisely spent. Unfortunately, the clash between those who see the defense budget as little more than an institutionalized anachronism, ripe for the picking to finance government initiatives in other sectors, and those who deny, as if by reflex, the possibility that there may be rational, lower-cost alternatives to the programs ordained by the Pentagon frequently impairs the objectivity of the debate this vital question quite properly inspires. Perhaps there can be no real way to determine how much military force is "enough." As with insurance, should the insured-against contingency actually occur, coverage seldom seems adequate. If it does not, one cannot help feeling that at least part of the premium might well have been better spent. But in addition to the amount of national security insurance the United States needs, it is important to decide what kind of forces equipped with which weapons can most efficiently provide the coverage.

The United States is a technologically wealthy nation. Clearly, failure to exploit this comparative advantage in technological resources in structuring the military forces would be as foolish as such a failure in structuring industrial processes. It is just as clear that the United States has not

1

been derelict in this respect. American forces have become more reliant on weapons than the forces of any other country. This distinction has been achieved by a consistent adherence to what might be described as a strategy of "maximum technological substitution," the notion that each new bit of technical information should be incorporated in a usable weapon and distributed to the operating forces with the least possible delay. Now, the soaring costs of military hardware have led many to suspect that this philosophy has been carried too far.

Aircraft are perhaps the most technically sophisticated of all the common machines man has devised, and U.S. tactical warplanes are among the most complex of aircraft systems. They must be complex, and hence much more costly unit-for-unit than warplanes of other nations, because of the performance required to carry out the arduous missions U.S. doctrine emphasizes. These expensive qualities mean that the nation must make do with fewer of them within a finite budget. Moreover, the missions that make U.S. aircraft expensive to produce and operate may not be those likely to be most productive in the principal military contingencies that might have to be faced.

Since World War II the unit cost of producing a first-line U.S. tactical combat aircraft has doubled, on the average, once every four years. Part of this growth has been caused by inflation, but most is attributable to the growing size and technical complexity of the aircraft themselves and to the declining rate of production that necessarily follows the climb in unit costs. With barely an exception, the introduction of each new weapon system has been accompanied by protestations over rising costs from Congress and, increasingly, from concerned private citizens as well. Underlying these recurring cost shocks are two fundamental, enduring, and closely allied issues. The first is mission priorities (what should U.S. tactical air forces do and in what order?); the second is design philosophy (what kinds of aircraft should be procured to do these things?).

This paper makes no attempt to prescribe what changes should be made in mission emphasis or which new aircraft and missile systems should be procured and which should not. Rather its purpose is to explain how different positions on the issues of mission priorities, aircraft design philosophy, the pace of modernization, and force levels might be expressed in decisions related to the several major new weapons acquisition programs now under way, and to define the implications of such decisions on costs and capabilities in the years ahead. The apparent course under present policy is appraised, and four alternative force structures contrasted to it.

CHAPTER TWO

TECHNOLOGICAL SUBSTITUTION
IN THE ARMED FORCES

The influence of advances in scientific knowledge during this century on the way ordinary goods and services are produced is well appreciated within the industrial societies. Better understanding of the workings of the physical world has, through the means of improved technology, proffered seemingly endless opportunity to gain new levels of efficiency by replacing direct human labor with the work of machines. Virtually every activity organized to transform resources has been affected. In most cases the spur has been strictly economic—a straightforward desire to produce more at lower cost—and the success that has been achieved is incontestable, evident to all in the decline in average costs of production.

Waging war is no different in principle from any resource transformation process, and should be just as eligible for the improvements in efficiency that have accrued elsewhere from technological substitution. If anything, automation within the military would seem to have a greater impetus than that which has motivated the process in other areas where human labor is consumed gradually and more or less figuratively. This is the special premium that many societies, including, certainly, our own, place on the lives of their soldiers.[1]

Shooting More and Fighting Less

It has become an accepted practice to view the ratio of combat to support forces as a gross indicator of the overall level of efficiency of the military organization (the higher the ratio, the more efficient the organiza-

1. American domestic reaction to the war in Southeast Asia attests to this. Although by no means indifferent to the drain on material resources, public concern focused much more intensely on U.S. casualties and, as casualty rates dwindled, the fate of prisoners of war than on dollar expenditures. The Vietnamization program and, more generally, the Nixon Doctrine's emphasis on the combination of U.S.

tion). By this standard the decline in the combat–support ratio from the pre-Vietnam ratio has been interpreted by many analysts as a sure sign of creeping bureaucratic inefficiency within the armed forces, which must be promptly redressed by cutting back the support "tail." While it would be foolish to challenge the contention that there are many support areas where savings could be realized at little or no sacrifice to overall mission effectiveness (in what large organization is this not the case?),[2] a high combat–support ratio is not necessarily a valid reflection of organizational efficiency. Nor is the fact that it is shrinking a prima facie cause for alarm or call for corrective action.

The combat–support ratio has actually been declining for at least a hundred years. This parallels a similar trend in the civilian work force— the acknowledged and generally applauded consequence of technological substitution in the economy as a whole. In 1940, for example, 38 percent of nonfarm, nonservice workers in the United States had occupations concerned primarily with carrying out some sort of manual operation. By 1950 this group of direct laborers had shrunk to 34 percent of the work force, and by 1970 to 22 percent.[3] Steady gains in overall productivity accompanied this redistribution of civilian occupations, and few would think to cite the shift as symbolic of declining industrial efficiency.

The direct labor of war is performed by the combat operatives— infantrymen, tank crews, artillerymen, fighter and bomber crewmen, and fighting ships' personnel—whose primary duty entails direct contact in battle with their counterparts on the other side. In the Army, where the bulk of U.S. combat manpower is concentrated, 36 percent of all personnel were combat troops during World War II; by the time of the Korean War this proportion had fallen to 33 percent, and in 1973 it was only 22 percent.[4] In all the services fewer than one out of every six persons in

---

technical resources and allied manpower to deter future conflict suggests that this distinction in real social cost between dollars and lives has not gone unrecognized.

2. Some analysts have concluded that the opportunities for realizing efficiency savings in support areas are particularly plentiful at present because of a tendency on the part of the military to make proportionately heavier reductions in mission forces than in the support infrastructure during periods when overall force levels are contracting, as in the past few years with the phasing down from the peak level reached during the war in Southeast Asia.

3. U.S. Bureau of the Census, *Statistical Abstract of the United States* (1949), pp. 179–86; and ibid. (1971), p. 222.

4. U.S. Army, "The Army: FY73" (declassified study; processed), p. C-3. The distinction between "combat" and "support" forces is not always crisp. The strictest definition is used here: personnel with a military occupational specialty (MOS) that has no civilian parallel.

uniform—360,000 of 2,200,000—currently serve in a combat specialty. (By way of historical comparison, better than nine of every ten persons serving in the Union forces during the American Civil War had combat specialties.) Rather than being symbolic of bureaucratic encroachment, the shift in military specialties away from those involving a combat function probably reflects the continuing process of substituting the firepower and mobility of improved war machines for manpower in battle: in short, military automation.

Data on the rate of consumption of munitions add support to the hypothesis that the United States has come to rely more on weapons in war and less on direct human participation and also manifest the growing importance of air-delivered firepower in this substitution process. Table 2-1 compares the aggregate inputs of manpower and firepower for World War II, Korea, and Southeast Asia. Measured against the estimated total military man-years of war effort, the rate at which munitions were

Table 2-1. The Trend in U.S. Battle Inputs, Manpower versus Firepower

Item	World War II (1941–45)	Korea (1950–53)	Southeast Asia (fiscal 1966–71)
Scale of war effort (millions of man-years)[a]	31.4	6.0	9.7
Combat exposure (millions of man-years)[a]	6.2	0.4	0.5
Munitions expended (millions of tons)	6.96	3.13	12.92
Surface-delivered	3.94	2.11	6.59
Air-delivered	3.02[b]	1.02	6.33[c]
Rate of munitions expenditure (tons per man-year of war effort)	0.2	0.5	1.3
Ratio of battle inputs (tons of munitions to man-years of combat exposure)	1–1	8–1	26–1

Sources: *Impact of the Vietnam War*, prepared by the Congressional Research Service for the Senate Committee on Foreign Relations, 92 Cong. 1 sess. (1971), pp. 8–9; Boston *Globe*, March 24, 1972; U.S. Navy, "Combat Activity of Naval Operations, April–July 1953" (prepared for the Chief of Naval Operations, April 1, 1954; processed); Office of the Assistant Secretary of Defense (comptroller), Directorate of Information Operations, *Selected Manpower Statistics* (1970), pp. 7, 21, 53, and unpublished tables; Department of the Army, "Pocket Data Book Supplement, 1968" (unclassified study prepared by the Comptroller of the Army; processed), p. 52; Office of the Assistant Secretary of Defense for Public Affairs, "Department of Defense Fact Sheet" (March 1972; processed), p. 17.

a. Author's estimates.

b. Includes 1.51 million tons delivered by strategic air forces against industrial, transportation, and population centers.

c. Includes 2.24 million tons delivered by B-52s against tactical targets.

expended in Southeast Asia was well over twice that for the Korean War and roughly six times the rate in World War II.[5]

The ascendancy of weapons over warriors in battle becomes still more apparent when munitions consumption is compared to the input of combat manpower. During World War II American forces expended roughly one ton of munitions for each year served in an operational theater by a combat-rated person. In Korea the comparable statistic was eight tons, and in Southeast Asia it soared to twenty-six tons. Moreover, these figures fail to allow for the improved effectiveness of modern munitions, in terms both of increased lethality and, in at least some instances, of accuracy.

The Human Savings

In Southeast Asia the rate at which casualties were sustained by U.S. ground combat forces (maneuver battalions) was fifteen times the average rate for support units that were not regularly exposed to the hazards of a battle environment. In a more conventional conflict, wherein battle zones would be better defined and rear areas possibly more secure than was the case in Vietnam, the disparity in casualty rates between combat and support units could be even more pronounced. Any innovation that produces a shift in the distribution of manpower away from high-casualty combat units into low-casualty support units, as has been the effect of technological substitution, therefore carries an implicit promise of fewer total casualties for a given force in a given period of time.

Data on U.S. casualty rates confirm that this is in fact the case.[6] Table 2-2 indicates that the overall rate of battle casualties in Korea declined by one-fourth from that in World War II and that the rate in

5. The analysis here is based on the assumption that World War II claimed in entirety the services of every man on active duty during the hostilities. The wars in Korea and Southeast Asia were no more than partial efforts, however, with many military personnel engaged in routine duties totally independent of the war in progress, making the "war effort" less than the total of man-years served (9.8 million during the Korean War; 19.2 million from fiscal 1966 to 1971). The war effort estimates for Korea and Southeast Asia are necessarily author's approximations. Any error would not be large enough to affect the general conclusion discussed in this paper, however.

6. It should be noted that demonstrating that casualty *rates* have declined does not prove conclusively that the human cost of war has lessened for the United States, only that lives were spent less quickly.

Table 2-2. U.S. Battle Casualties

Number and rate	World War II (1941–45)	Korea (1950–53)	Southeast Asia (fiscal 1966–71)
Casualties (thousands)	962.4	136.9	191.2
Battle deaths	291.6	33.6	44.0
Wounds not mortal[a]	670.8	103.3	147.2
Rate per thousand			
man-years of war effort	30.7	22.8	19.7
Battle deaths	9.3	5.6	4.5
Wounds not mortal[a]	21.4	17.2	15.2

Sources: Bureau of the Census, *Statistical Abstract of the United States* (1971), p. 251; James D. Hessman, "U.S. Combat Deaths Drop 90% as Vietnamization Takes Hold," *Armed Forces Journal* (April 1972), pp. 42–44. See also Table 2-1, above.
a. Includes only wounds requiring hospital treatment. Improved reporting procedures in Southeast Asia enabled the recording of minor wounds in that conflict not recorded in earlier wars.

Southeast Asia was more than 10 percent lower than in Korea. In other words, had the World War II rate prevailed in Southeast Asia, the United States would have suffered at least 100,000 more killed and wounded in battle than the 191,200 actually recorded between July 1, 1965, and June 30, 1971.

One explanation frequently put forth to account for declining casualty rates is improvements in evacuation and medical treatment. Although this is no doubt reflected in the decreasing proportion of fatalities among battle casualties (in that many who would previously have died of their wounds are now saved by prompt treatment), it cannot explain the downward trend in the overall rate of killed and wounded. On the contrary, the ready availability of medical attention in Vietnam may well have inflated that war's overall battle casualty statistics, since many of the less seriously wounded in Vietnam—who would of necessity have been treated in the field in World War II or Korea and thus gone uncounted—were evacuated to rear areas for hospital care and thereby entered the accounting system.

It is also argued that the casualty rates for Southeast Asia are not directly comparable to the rates in World War II or the Korean War because the enemy's tactics in Southeast Asia differed so greatly from the conventional set-piece encounters typical of the earlier wars. Certainly, the casualty rate in a modern conventional war against an opponent armed with sophisticated weaponry would be expected to exceed that of Vietnam. But it can also be argued that the communists' tactics in Southeast Asia, which featured widely dispersed, constantly maneuvering small-unit operations and only occasional brief force concentrations, were imposed on them by the overwhelming superiority of U.S. firepower. If intensive use of technology in war by the United States compels technologically poor opponents to adopt tactics that further reduce U.S. casualty rates, so much the better.

Proving Cost-Effectiveness

Although the potential for reducing battle casualties may be the strongest argument for continuing the traditional U.S. philosophy of pressing the limits of technology in weapons development and procurement, the usual test in deciding whether a specific new system should be procured is that of dollars-and-cents cost-effectiveness. Does the new system offer enough extra capability to justify its (typically) greater cost? Even with the simplest weapon systems, a precise answer to this straightforward question can prove tantalizingly elusive. With complex systems such as tactical warplanes, concrete conclusions about economic justification are seldom if ever attainable. In this atmosphere of uncertainty the traditional practice of the United States in equipping its military forces seems to award the benefit of the doubt to innovation and the new weapon.

Because of the singular difficulty the analyst encounters in trying to measure military "output" (or even in finding a quantifiable definition of what it is that U.S. armed forces produce[7]), it cannot be demonstrated conclusively that this approach has been economic, let alone optimal. Obviously it has not led to lower defense budgets or fewer men in uniform. But this constitutes no proof of diseconomy either, for whatever dividends may have accrued along the way may have been reinvested in higher military capacity, rather than paid out in the form of dollar reductions in the defense budget.

There is only a roundabout way to appraise the efficiency question. This is by placing a hypothetical equal-cost trade-off in a broad historical context. To deny that the steady introduction of increasingly complex weaponry has led toward greater economic efficiency, one would have to argue that a more formidable military posture would be achieved if the $63 billion to be spent on general purpose forces this year were invested in forces organized and equipped as they were in 1953, 1945, or 1918

---

7. This is not to imply that U.S. military forces produce nothing of value. Their final product, national security, clearly yields essential social utility in an adversary world. The problem is that security is an abstraction that cannot itself be measured and that may be no more than vaguely related to the intermediate goods of war—enemy casualties, rate of advance of the forward edge of the battle area, blue sorties on red forces, etc.—that are subject, at least conceptually, to quantification.

rather than by today's standards. It seems safe to presume that very few would support such a policy.

Although the way in which the armed forces have applied technological progress in the past may have been cost-effective on the whole, this does not mean that the same strategy is the best one for meeting current problems.

Air Power's Part

As the firepower of American armed forces has increased, so has reliance on the airplane as the means of delivery. From fiscal 1966 through 1971, when a substantial number of U.S. ground forces were in Vietnam, nearly half the total weight of munitions expended by all U.S. forces in Southeast Asia was delivered by air. In the Korean War air-delivered munitions constituted about one-third of the total. And in World War II the comparable fraction for munitions expended against tactical targets was only slightly greater than one-fourth.[8]

As noted, the application of technology to replace manpower with machine power in battle has led to a shift in the combination of battle inputs, and this has been in large measure responsible for the long-diminishing ratio of combat-to-support personnel within the U.S. military organization, resulting in lower overall casualty rates. All of these—the combination of battle inputs, the combat–support ratio, and the casualty rate—show the central importance of the tactical air forces' role in the general trend described as technological substitution.

The impact of air power on the combination of battle inputs, which is estimated (Table 2-1) to have averaged 26 tons of munitions for each man-year of combat exposure for all U.S. forces in Southeast Asia, is readily demonstrated. From fiscal 1966 to 1971 the average quantity of munitions delivered in one attack sortie by a fighter-bomber was 2.0 tons.[9] If it is conservatively assumed that each aircraft carried a two-man crew (many had only one man) and the few minutes actually spent in a combat

8. The World War II total of just under 7 million tons for all U.S. forces (see Table 2-1) includes 1.5 million tons used in strategic air bombardment—a mission carried out on a much lesser scale in Korea and not at all (at least formally) during the six-year period from which the data on Southeast Asia were drawn. The distinction between strategic and tactical missions is discussed in chapter 5.

9. *Fiscal Year 1974 Authorization for Military Procurement . . .* , Hearings before the Senate Armed Services Committee, 93 Cong. 1 sess. (1973), part 1, pp. 427–34.

environment on the attack passes are counted as a full day's combat exposure for each man, battle inputs for fighter-bomber operations in Southeast Asia were at the rate of 365 tons of munitions for each man-year of combat exposure.

For the tactical strike operations carried out by modified B-52 bombers carrying five- or six-man crews and delivering an average of 24.8 tons of munitions on each sortie, the ratio of firepower to manpower was far greater—more than 1,500 tons of firepower for each man-year of combat exposure (in, it should be noted, a very low-risk environment).[10]

Inclusion of the additional combat exposure of other personnel engaged in direct support activities, such as forward air controllers and the aircrews of reconnaissance and rescue aircraft, would lower these ratios somewhat, but it remains clear that the mixture of battle inputs achieved through the use of tactical air power is far richer in firepower than that for the surface forces, which, taken alone, supported each man-year of combat exposure in Southeast Asia with about 13 tons of munitions.

The capital-intensive quality of U.S. tactical air forces is further shown by their extremely low ratio of combat to support personnel. The Army, for example, has a combat–support ratio of roughly 1–5 whereas the tactical air components of the Air Force, Navy, and Marine Corps have a ratio of about 1–70 (about 340,000 persons supporting an operational strength of 2,700 fighter and attack aircraft, or an average of more than 120 persons for each warplane).

Although the data available are not adequate to isolate the casualty rate for the combined tactical air components of the three services, the overall Air Force rate probably provides a reasonable (if somewhat inflated because of the sanctuary enjoyed by the personnel supporting the sea-based operations) approximation. Air Force personnel contributed an estimated 1.3 million to 1.5 million man-years (about 15 percent of the total) to the U.S. war effort in Southeast Asia in fiscal years 1966–71 while suffering 1,528 battle casualties, 779 of which were fatalities. The overall Air Force casualty rate was therefore not more than 1.2 per thousand man-years, or about one-sixteenth the rate at which casualties were sustained by all U.S. forces.

---

10. Aside from firepower, technological substitution tends to displace combat manpower by increasing the efficiency with which the basic inputs to war, capital and labor, can be managed. This is made possible by offering improved intelligence, communications, and mobility to those in command. Although these managerial factors will not be treated in depth in this paper, their relevance to the substitution process should be recognized.

CHAPTER THREE

THE PRESENT COURSE

In his first inaugural address President Nixon promised a new foreign policy that would lead the United States out of a period of confrontation into a period of negotiation. On the military side the strategy for bringing this about, which has become known as the "Nixon Doctrine," stresses three points: first, the United States will continue to honor its treaty commitments; second, it will provide a shield against the threat of nuclear powers for nations whose survival is deemed vital to American interests; and third, in cases of conventional aggression it will provide appropriate assistance upon request but will "look to the nation directly threatened to assume the primary responsibility of providing manpower for its defense."

One interpretation of this last point sees in it a declaration of U.S. intent to rely still more heavily on the technology-intensive modes of military power to deter, and if necessary fight, future conflicts. This in turn may be taken to signal a boom in tactical air power, both land- and sea-based. The course of events in Southeast Asia, where the tempo of U.S. air operations continued unabated and in some ways actually intensified well after the land war had been thoroughly "Vietnamized," and U.S. policy toward South Korea, where from 1970 on the Nixon administration hinted that the last of the American ground combat troops would eventually be withdrawn and their deterrence function transferred in large part to the tactical air forces, both lend credence to this view.

On the other hand, the most demanding military contingency the United States might have to face would be an attack by the Warsaw Pact countries on its NATO allies, and there is no indication that U.S. ground forces will play a significantly smaller role in this. Quite the contrary: the Nixon administration steadfastly opposed unilaterally cutting these forces in Europe, and President Ford in his August 1974 address to a joint session of Congress strongly stressed continuity in foreign policy and defense matters.

11

Budget considerations also argue against any absolute increase in emphasis on tactical air power at this time. Such a policy would encounter not only the general resistance to larger defense budgets that has developed during a period when international tensions in most areas of the world have been subsiding while a multitude of domestic demands compete for public resources, but also the special aversion many feel toward the extremely high cost of modern, ultrasophisticated military aircraft.

With the emerging generation of fighter aircraft, the problem of rising unit costs has reached proportions that will make it impossible to preserve both the numerical level and the long-range offensive character of the present forces throughout the 1970s without either severely curtailing their customary rate of modernization or dramatically increasing the major weapons investment portion of the tactical air budget—to as much as double the current pace of $5 billion a year. How to balance the level of forces, the kinds of aircraft with which they are equipped, and the rate at which they are modernized against the pressures to contain the defense budget is the most difficult problem planners for the tactical air forces now face.

The course of present policy in striking this balance is clear only for the next two or three years. The projection is for roughly constant budgets and force levels through fiscal year 1978, with the cost of procuring the expensive new fighters financed largely by slowing the pace of modernization. That is, the high unit cost of these systems will be offset by acquiring fewer of them.

Beyond this, the course of present policy becomes far more difficult to chart as it is likely to depend on decisions not yet formed. Before the large procurement programs now under way begin to expire in 1978 and 1979, a fundamental choice will have to be made. Briefly put, the options will be three: to continue these programs at the same pace, thereby holding the budget in check but accepting the inevitability of lower force levels in the 1980s as operating attrition reduces the aging force; to permit the programs to phase down as scheduled, redirecting the procurement moneys freed by this action to the acquisition of less expensive kinds of aircraft in larger quantities, thereby preserving force levels but altering the relative mission capabilities of the forces; or to provide the substantial infusion of new funds necessary to expand the established programs sufficiently to allow full modernization with aircraft such as the F-14 and F-15.[1]

1. The modernization problem is especially acute for the Navy, which not only has selected the more costly design for its air wings, but must also allow for the fact that two-thirds of its aircraft carriers were built in rapid succession during the 1950s

The rest of this chapter will be devoted to describing the plans laid out by the Defense Department in testimony before Congress and to projecting the way in which these plans are likely to shape the structure and costs of the tactical air forces in the next five years.

Force Levels

Barring the unlikely event of a negotiated agreement for mutual limitations on the size of the major powers' general purpose forces, the level of U.S. tactical air forces is apt to change little during the remainder of the 1970s under current policy. The number of Navy carrier air wings (CVWs) may be expected to decline by two from the current level of fourteen by 1980 as age reduces the size of the carrier fleet to twelve ships. Although not indicated at this time, a further reduction in the number of CVWs stemming from doctrinal revisions now being tested that will assign each carrier dual responsibility for antisubmarine and attack operations remains a possibility. Three large nuclear-powered carriers will join the fleet by the end of fiscal 1980 or 1981; five attack carriers of World War II vintage will reach the customary retirement age of thirty years.[2] In addition, three old ships modified for antisubmarine warfare (ASW) will be scrapped and not replaced.[3]

Because the new carriers are much larger than those that will be retired, the aggregate operational capacity of the attack carrier fleet, as measured by the number of representative A-4 aircraft that could be accommodated aboard all the ships in commission, will decrease by barely 2 percent (from 1,678 at the end of fiscal 1974 to 1,644 in 1980). More than off-

---

and will require replacement at the same rate during the 1980s if the size of the fleet is to be maintained.

2. In his Annual Defense Department Report for 1975, Secretary James R. Schlesinger announced a temporary expansion in the number of attack carriers from fourteen in 1974 to fifteen by the end of fiscal 1975. This is a departure from earlier plans (which had indicated a twelve-ship force by this time) achieved by delaying the retirement of two Essex-class ships (one of which, the *Hancock*, is already past the usual thirty-year retirement age) and one ship of the Midway class while the first ship of the new Nimitz class joins the line. These three older ships and two additional ships of the Midway class must be retired by the end of the decade, however. With only two additional Nimitz-class carriers under construction, this leads to a twelve-ship force in the early 1980s.

3. Under the "CV" conversion program, the three ASW air wings displaced from these ships will be distributed among the attack carriers in varying numbers geared to prevailing operational requirements.

setting this slight decline, four of the ships in the 1980 force will have the far greater cruising endurance and ranging latitude that nuclear power provides—advantages the Navy believes are well worth the $300-odd million in extra construction costs for each such ship. Only one of the carriers in the present force has these capabilities. On the other hand, as much as 15 percent of the capacity of the 1980 fleet could be absorbed in carrying out antisubmarine operations now delegated to the three ASW carriers that will be phased out without replacement.

Air Force strength is also likely to remain near the present level of twenty-one fighter-attack wings, although the possibility that as many as six wings equipped with specialized A-10 attack aircraft may be added to this strength cannot be ruled out. Marine Corps tactical air strength is expected to remain at three wings indefinitely.

Table 3-1 compares the current and projected organizational levels of the three services to past levels. A more detailed presentation, indicating present and projected squadron counts by type of aircraft, appears in Appendix A.

Table 3-1. Active Fighter and Attack Forces, by Number of Wings and Squadrons, Selected Fiscal Years, 1961–80

Fiscal year	Air Force[a]		Navy		Marine Corps[b]	
	Wings	Squadrons	Wings	Squadrons	Wings	Squadrons
1961	20	61	17	84	3	28
1964	24	73	17	85	3	28
1968[c]	27	81	16	78	3	27
1972	23	70	13	66	3	27
1974	21	64	14	70	3	28
1975[d]	21	65	14	71	3	28
1980[d]	22	66	12	63	3	30

Source: Author's estimates.
a. Excludes fighter designs modified for electronic warfare operations. There are currently four such squadrons; an increase to seven is projected for fiscal 1980.
b. Includes three squadrons of helicopter gunships in fiscal 1972 and thereafter.
c. Excludes sixteen reserve squadrons temporarily on active duty and eight air defense interceptor squadrons temporarily transferred to tactical service. These units have been returned to reserve status.
d. Projected.

The organizational strength of tactical elements of the reserve forces should also remain very close to present levels throughout the 1970s. At the end of fiscal 1974 the reserves had a combined strength of 132 tactical squadrons, 48 of which were equipped with fighter or attack aircraft. These units were distributed among the reserves as follows:[4]

4. "Other aircraft" include reconnaissance, electronic warfare, airlift, special

	Fighter or attack aircraft	Other aircraft	Total
Air National Guard	27	41	68
Air Force Reserve	3	34	37
Naval Air Reserve	10	2	12
Marine Reserve Air Wing	8	7	15

Although wing or squadron counts are the most common means of expressing force levels, because these units are not homogeneous their total can sometimes be misleading.[5] A more accurate indicator of size is reached by counting the number of aircraft the operating units are authorized to have. In technical parlance this is referred to as "unit equipment" strength. Under most circumstances it is the best way to estimate the number of airplanes that would be available on short notice for wartime use. Table 3-2 compares past, present, and projected fighter and attack force levels by this standard.

The unit equipment strength of the tactical air combat forces has not varied by much more than 5 percent in either direction since the beginning of the 1960s—a considerably lesser fluctuation than that of the squadron count. Comparable stability can be anticipated for the rest of the 1970s. The unit equipment strength of the noncombat forces, which include

---

operating forces, aerial refueling, observation, and rescue types. The Navy total does not include ASW types.

5. Neither the number of aircraft in a squadron nor the number of squadrons in a wing is consistent either among or within the services. Most Air Force tactical fighter wings (TFWs) are authorized to contain 72 aircraft, organized into three squadrons of 24 aircraft apiece. But some Air Force squadrons still retain the old authorized strength of the 1960s—18 aircraft. (By the end of fiscal 1976 all these squadrons will have 24 aircraft.) A TFW composed of three such squadrons therefore has only 54 aircraft, all of which are of the same basic design (e.g., F-4s, F-111s, or A-7s). Navy carrier air wings (CVWs) normally have five squadrons of 12 aircraft each, three equipped with attack aircraft (one "heavy" and two "light") and two with fighter designs. CVWs operating from the new Nimitz-class carriers will, however, be boosted to a fighter-attack authorization of 72 aircraft by the addition of a fourth squadron of light attack types. In addition each CVW is assigned 12 to 20 noncombat aircraft to conduct reconnaissance, electronic warfare, aerial refueling, early warning, antisubmarine, resupply, and search and rescue functions for the carrier task force. Marine air wings have an authorized strength of about 320 aircraft, roughly half of which are unarmed helicopters. Combat strength consists of about 140 fixed-wing fighter-attack aircraft, organized in nine squadrons (four fighter and five attack), and one squadron of helicopter gunships, which, on the Marine Corps's initiative, replaced a sixth light attack squadron in each wing during the second half of the 1960s. The authorized strength of Marine squadrons varies from 20 to 12 aircraft depending on the complexity, and hence maintenance burden, of the design with which a squadron is equipped.

Table 3-2. Unit Equipment Strength of Active Fighter and Attack Forces, Selected Fiscal Years, 1961–80

Fiscal year	Air Force	Navy	Marine Corps	Total
1961	1,290	950	600	2,840
1964	1,500	990	520	3,010
1968[a]	1,620	870	440	2,930
1972	1,500	790	400	2,690
1974	1,440	850	430	2,720
1975[b]	1,530	860	430	2,820
1980[b]	1,580	760	470	2,810

Source: Author's estimates. Figures are rounded.
a. Excludes 314 aircraft in activated reserve squadrons and approximately 120 interceptors transferred from strategic air defense forces.
b. Projected.

reconnaissance and electronic aircraft, fixed-wing and (in the Marine Corps) helicopter transports, tankers for aerial refueling, and search and rescue and light observation types, should also remain almost constant, in the range of 1,700 to 1,900 aircraft. Since both sets of forces will be aging during this period, in the absence of either increased investment spending or a decision to change the kinds of airplanes being procured, shrinking levels will be unavoidable after 1980.[6]

Although counting airplanes is preferable to counting wings or squadrons as a means of measuring force levels, this method also suffers from the shortcoming that not all the things being tallied are alike. In 1975, for example, the United States will have very nearly the same number of aircraft in operational squadrons as it had in 1961, before the buildup in conventional forces that accompanied the "doctrine of flexible response" during the early Kennedy-McNamara years. But less than 7 percent of the 1974 force is equipped with aircraft of the same basic design as those in the 1961 force, and all of these are later models with significantly improved performance. Better than 93 percent of the present combat force is equipped with aircraft designs introduced since 1960 that incorporate still greater qualitative gains. Clearly, improved unit performance ought not to be ignored. The problem is how to accurately weigh the effect such qualitative changes have had on force capacity.[7]

6. Using surplus aircraft procured in earlier years, the Air Force is converting its remaining 18 UE (unit equipment) F-4 squadrons to 24 UE strength. Twelve of the smaller squadrons will be upgraded in fiscal 1975 (increasing total UE strength by 72 aircraft), and the last four will be upgraded in fiscal 1976. One 24 UE F-15 squadron will be added to the force in fiscal 1975.

7. Moreover, the true measure of sufficiency is not merely capacity, it is capability: what U.S. forces can be expected to achieve against a given array of opposing

There can be no simple, and there is no unanimously accepted, technique for doing so. However, it might be noted that some of the most significant improvements in the performance of U.S. combat designs in recent years have been in the form of greater range and payload-carrying ability. In the process the aircraft have grown much larger and heavier, suggesting that the gross weight of the fighter-attack armada might be a better indicator of its size than the number of aircraft in it (a similar concept, "standard displacement," has for many years been an accepted, though imperfect, standard for measuring the size of naval fleets) and that the contributions of technological progress would become still more apparent if the aggregate lift capacity of the evolving force was measured. Within broad limits, increases in what an airplane can lift (in addition to its own weight) can be used to carry additional fuel, which extends range, avionics, which improve penetration capability and strike accuracy, or munitions, which add firepower. In any case the offensive potential of the system becomes greater.[8] Not all such gains are absolute, however. Additional electronics equipment, for example, may be required merely to offset improved air defenses. And lift capacity alone is of limited use as an indicator of a design's potency in aerial combat.

Although these caveats should be kept in mind, by either index—weight of aircraft or lift capacity—the active fighter and attack forces expanded rapidly during the 1960s and early 1970s but are expected to decline slightly over the five-year forecast period as the number of F-4s and F-111s declines.[9] As shown in Table 3-3, the aggregate weight of the aircraft in U.S. active combat forces in 1975 stands at a modern high, 40 percent above the 1961 level. And lift capacity, benefiting from technological advances that have increased the lift–weight ratio of modern designs (the average aircraft in 1961 could lift less than 0.8 pound for each

---

forces. Gains in the capacity of U.S. forces need not be proportionate gains in capability if the other side's capacity, in this case for air defense, is also expanding.

8. A desirable refinement would be to consider sortie rates as well, since they vary considerably for different aircraft—generally in an inverse relation to design complexity—and are also sensitive to such other factors as maintenance manning levels and the availability of support equipment.

9. The empty weight of the F-4 is 28,000 pounds; its lift capacity is 26,400 pounds. The empty weights of the first models of the F-14 and the F-15 are estimated to be 37,000 pounds and 28,000 pounds respectively; the lift capacity of both designs is almost 20,000 pounds (a figure likely to increase substantially for later models). Replacing F-4s with F-14s and F-15s consequently reduces aggregate lift capacity, as does the projected conversion of one wing of F-111 fighter-bombers to an electronic warfare configuration.

Table 3-3. Aggregate Weight and Lift Capacity of Active Fighter and Attack Forces,
Selected Fiscal Years, 1961–80

Millions of pounds

Characteristic	1961	1964	1968ª	1972	1974	1975ᵇ	1980ᵇ
*Weight of aircraft*ᶜ							
Air Force	29.1	35.5	42.5	44.7	46.4	47.0	45.3
Navy	15.2	17.2	14.9	17.3	19.4	19.9	19.0
Marine Corps	8.0	8.2	9.2	7.5	8.5	8.6	9.3
Total	52.3	60.9	66.6	69.5	74.3	75.5	73.6
*Lift capacity*ᵈ							
Air Force	20.9	27.8	36.9	42.7	45.2	45.7	43.0
Navy	12.4	16.2	17.1	19.9	20.9	21.1	18.0
Marine Corps	7.0	8.1	9.8	8.1	8.7	8.6	9.4
Total	40.3	52.1	63.8	70.7	74.8	75.4	70.4

Source: Author's estimates.
a. Excludes temporarily activated reserve units and transfers from Aerospace Defense Command.
b. Projected.
c. Aggregate weight—empty weight of aircraft authorized for operational squadrons.
d. Aggregate lift capacity—maximum takeoff weight less empty weight of aircraft authorized for operational squadrons.

pound of its own weight whereas the average airplane in the 1974 force can lift 1.0 pound), is nearly twice as great as it was in 1961. Moreover another 20 million pounds of fighter and attack aircraft with 16 million pounds of lift capacity are assigned to the reserves. Modernization of these forces is likely by 1980 to increase their present aggregate lift capacity by 20 to 30 percent.

Figure 3-1 shows the different trends resulting from the different measurements of force levels discussed above.

Still another way to gauge force levels is by the total inventory of active aircraft. Because of backup requirements for training and maintenance and the policy of buying a store of aircraft to replace those expected to be lost through accident and ordinary peacetime wear and tear, the number of aircraft of a particular design a service has usually exceeds the unit equipment strength of its operating squadrons by 50 percent or more.[10] Few of the backup aircraft are available for operational duties on short

10. When a new design is introduced, the number of aircraft procured is ordinarily 70 to 80 percent greater than the unit equipment strength that has been planned. For older designs that are nearing the end of their service life and are no longer in production, aircraft inventory may fall to no more than 20 or 30 percent above unit equipment strength. See "F-111s Prove Worth in Southeast Asia," *Armed Forces Journal* (March 1973), p. 22.

Figure 3-1. Number of Squadrons and Unit Equipment Aircraft, Weight, and Lift Capacity of Active Fighter and Attack Forces, at End of Selected Fiscal Years, 1961–80[a]

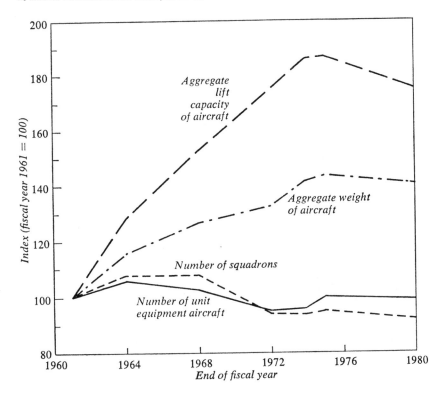

a. Curves from 1974 to 1980 are projected.

notice, but many could be pressed into service in a wartime emergency as replacements for combat losses.

The total active aircraft inventory of the services has declined appreciably since 1961. For the active duty components of the Air Force, an inventory of 8,300 aircraft of all types is planned for the end of fiscal 1974, 46 percent fewer than in 1961. Since 1970 the rate of decline in the active aircraft inventory has been particularly steep, averaging 5.1 percent annually. Much of the drop may be attributed to post-Vietnam realignments, however, as evidenced by the tapering off in the rate of decline during 1974, shown in Table 3-4, which also shows that the inventory reductions have fallen more heavily on the active than on the reserve forces, and more heavily on the Air Force than on the Navy or Marine Corps. It is

Table 3-4. Inventory of Active Aircraft, Fiscal Years 1970–74[a]

Service and type of aircraft	1970	1971	1972	1973	1974	Average annual change (percent)
Service						
Air Force	13,357	12,551	11,585	10,775	10,573	−5.7
Active	11,071	10,239	9,235	8,484	8,313	−6.4
Reserve	2,286	2,312	2,350	2,291	2,260	−0.3
Navy and Marine Corps	7,929	7,318	6,752	6,797	6,697	−4.1
Active	7,153	6,482	6,068	6,086	6,002	−4.2
Reserve	776	836	684	711	695	−2.2
Total[b]	21,286	19,869	18,337	17,572	17,270	−5.1
Type of aircraft[c]						
Tactical fighter and attack[d]	7,300	6,700	6,600	6,500	6,400	−3
All others	14,000	13,200	11,700	11,100	10,900	−6

Sources: *Department of Defense Appropriations*, Hearings before a Subcommittee of the House Committee on Appropriations, 92 Cong. 1 and 2 sess., 93 Cong. 1 sess., "Operations and Maintenance": *Fiscal Year 1972*, part 4, p. 19; *Fiscal Year 1973*, part 5, p. 16; *Fiscal Year 1974*, part 5, p. 16. *United States Military Posture for Fiscal Year 1974*, Report by the Chairman of the Joint Chiefs of Staff to the Senate Committee on Appropriations (1973), p. 34. Air Force Directorate of Management Analysis, *USAF Summary* (1973).

a. Does not include aircraft in allied air forces provided by the United States under the Military Assistance Program.

b. In addition the Army has about 9,600 aircraft, most of them helicopters.

c. Figures are rounded.

d. Includes electronic warfare and reconnaissance aircraft.

also noteworthy that tactical fighter, attack, and reconnaissance aircraft have declined at only half the rate for other types.

Within the Air Force the elements least affected by shrinking inventories were the strategic offense forces, which lost only thirty-one bombers and tankers between 1970 and 1974 (a reduction of 2.6 percent). The greatest proportionate reductions during the past four years occurred in the strategic defensive (interceptor) forces, which were reduced to fewer than 200 aircraft—a 60 percent reduction since 1970.[11] In 1960 the Air Force had nearly 1,600 interceptors. Airlift forces, both strategic and tactical, dropped by 425 aircraft, but the largest numerical reduction was in the area of training and support, which lost over 1,200 aircraft, or one-fourth its 1970 strength. The inventory of tactical fighter, attack, reconnaissance, and electronic warfare aircraft in the active-duty forces also

11. The responsibility for continental air defense against manned bombers now rests primarily with the Air National Guard, which has approximately 400 interceptors.

dropped by about one-fourth, from 3,983 in 1970 to 2,998 in 1974—a decline partially offset by an increase of about 150 such types in reserve components. Despite the recent reductions, the Air Force will have almost exactly the same number of fighter and attack aircraft on active duty at the end of fiscal 1974 as it had in 1961 (2,346 and 2,358 respectively). And qualitative gains should be kept in mind.

Each year during peacetime, operating attrition claims from 6 to 8 percent of the active aircraft inventory.[12] Therefore, the Air Force, Navy, and Marine Corps would have to procure more than 1,000 aircraft and helicopters this year to avoid any further diminution in the inventory in a year or two, when current orders will be delivered. But funds are requested in the 1975 budget to procure only 318 fixed-wing aircraft and 40 helicopters for all three services (288 of which are tactical types).[13] Last year, 418 aircraft and helicopters of all types, including 342 tactical types, were procured for use by these services.[14] A continuing decline in the total aircraft inventory of several hundred units a year consequently seems assured, at least through 1977. As has been the case in the first half of the decade, this shrinkage should affect the tactical forces less than other areas.

Past reductions have been mostly in the strategic defensive forces (readily justifiable in light of the diminishing importance of bombers in the strategic nuclear threat), the airlift forces (warranted by the substantial qualitative improvements in transport aircraft design), and the support forces (made possible by such managerial innovations as greater reliance on simulators for flight training and commercial carriers for routine transportation). The strategic defense forces are approaching the minimum needed for surveillance purposes, however, and aircraft inventories in the other areas that have produced procurement economies must eventually be stabilized as well. Thus these forces will soon cease to be a source of savings in aircraft procurement that can be used to finance the large programs under way to acquire new tactical warplanes and must begin to compete more vigorously for the funds being spent.

12. *Defense Authorizations for Fiscal Year 1972,* Hearings before the Senate Armed Services Committee, 92 Cong. 1 sess. (1971), part 1, p. 100. The hazards of operating over water and of carrier takeoffs and landings lead to a somewhat higher rate of operating attrition for the Navy than for the other services.

13. Procurement funding for an additional 42 aircraft was included in a supplemental request submitted at the same time as the 1975 budget. Many of these aircraft are needed to replace aircraft sent to Israel during 1974, however.

14. U.S. Department of Defense, *Program Acquisition Cost by Weapon System, Fiscal Year 1974* (1973), and *Fiscal Year 1975* (1974).

Table 3-5. Actual and Estimated Acquisition Costs of Major New Tactical Air Programs,[a] Various Fiscal Years
Billions of current dollars

System	1975 status	Description	Cost					Number in procurement program
			Through 1974	1975	1976–80	Total		
F-15	Early procurement	Multipurpose combat aircraft	3.06	1.08	5.9	10.0		729
F-14A	Procurement	Multipurpose combat aircraft	3.85	0.76	1.8	6.4		322
F-14B	Development	F-14A, upgraded with advanced engine	0.37	n.a.	0.1	0.5[b]		...
AIM-54A	Procurement	Air-to-air missile (for F-14)	0.64	0.10	0.5	1.2		2,457
AIM-7F	Early procurement	Air-to-air missile	0.18	0.10	0.7	1.0		7,500
AGM-53A	Procurement	Air-to-surface missile	0.23	0.03	0.6	0.8		n.a.
AWACS	Initial procurement	Warning and control aircraft	0.68	0.77	1.0	2.4		34
A-10	Initial procurement	Special purpose combat aircraft (close support)	0.20	0.27	2.1	2.6		729
LWF	Development	Special purpose combat aircraft (counterair)	0.10	0.02	0.1	0.2[b]		...
ACF	Initial development	Special purpose combat aircraft (counterair)	...	0.04	0.1	0.2[b]		...
AMST	Development	Multipurpose transport aircraft	0.06	0.06	0.1	0.2[b]		...
EF-111	Development	Electronic warfare aircraft	0.02	0.04	[c]	0.1[b]		...
AV-16	Initial development	Special purpose combat aircraft (close support)	0	0.01	0.3	0.3[b]		...
Total			9.39	3.28	13.3	25.9		...

Source: Author's estimates.
n.a. Not available.
a. Not fully operational as of March 1974.
b. Cost of the research and development program only. The procurement prospects and potentials for each of these systems, as well as the most likely candidates for totally new initiatives, are discussed in the text.
c. Less than 0.05.

New Weapons

The Defense Department's budget submission for 1975 requested funds to proceed with thirteen major programs to acquire new weapon systems for the tactical air forces. Procurement continues for another twelve major systems that already enjoy full operational status.[15] What each of these programs is currently estimated to cost and the number of units to be procured under the formal plans laid out by the Defense Department are shown in Tables 3-5 and 3-6.

In fiscal years 1975–80 investment in defined programs to modernize the tactical air forces with new aircraft and missiles will total $22 billion to $23 billion in current dollars. Initiatives to develop and procure further major weapon systems—such as new aircraft carriers, reconnaissance and possibly also attack versions of the F-14 and F-15, a new short-takeoff-and-landing (STOL) transport, and an improved follow-on to the AV-8 Harrier—as well as to extend the basic F-14, F-15, and A-10 programs with additional procurement of improved models (all efforts that, though not yet announced in most instances, are better than even prospects for the second half of the 1970s) may be expected to add at least $10 billion to the tactical air budget through 1980.

Although roughly five out of every six of these dollars will be spent on systems that are not yet operational, two-thirds of the active combat forces will still be equipped in 1980 with aircraft of the same basic design as those in today's arsenal. The F-4, a design that first flew in 1958, will still be relied on for nearly 60 percent of the air combat capability. As shown in Table 3-7, the projected pace of modernization for the rest of the 1970s is slower than the pace achieved during the 1960s. Only the Air Force will come close to matching previous modernization experience.

Throughout the forecast period, investment in major weapon systems will continue to be dominated by a pair of new long-range fighters, the Air Force's F-15 Eagle and the Navy's F-14 Tomcat. Approximately $10 billion remains to be obligated for completing the programs the Defense Department has laid out for acquiring the two systems. For reasons discussed below it is highly probable that the requests for funds to support the F-14 and F-15 will rise well above this level, however, possibly to twice the announced amount by the end of fiscal 1980, thereby consuming nearly two-thirds of the modernization budget projected for this period.

15. Congress has appropriated unrequested funds to procure additional F-111s and A-7Ds (the Air Force version) for the past several years and may do so again in fiscal 1975.

Table 3-6. Actual and Estimated Acquisition Costs of Major Established Tactical Air Programs,[a] Various Fiscal Years
Billions of current dollars

System	Description	Cost				Number in procurement program
		Through 1974	1975	1976–80	Total	
F-4E	Multipurpose combat aircraft	2.53	0.02	[b]	2.6	812
F-5E/F	Special purpose combat aircraft (counterair)[c]	0.47	0.11	0.4	1.0	320
F-111	Multipurpose combat aircraft	7.16	0	0	7.2	461[d]
A-4M	Light attack aircraft	0.26	0.07	0.4	0.7	220[e]
A-6E	Heavy attack aircraft	0.64	0.14	1.2	2.0	192
A-7D	Light attack aircraft (Air Force)	1.58	0	0	1.6	435[f]
A-7E	Light attack aircraft (Navy)	1.68	0.16	1.2	3.0	706
AH-1J	Attack helicopter	0.13	0.03	[b]	0.2	120[e]
EA-6B	Electronic warfare aircraft	1.04	0.13	0.8	2.0	90[e]
E-2C	Warning and control aircraft	0.86	0.12	0.5	1.5	60[e]
C-130E/H	Multipurpose transport aircraft	1.30	0.04	[b]	1.4	453
AIM-9H/L	Air-to-air missile	0.11	0.02	0.1	0.2	n.a.
AGM-45A	Air-to-surface missile	0.23	0.04	0.1	0.4	n.a.
AGM-65	Air-to-surface missile	0.37	0.11	0.2	0.6	n.a.
Total		18.36	0.99	4.9	24.4	

Source: Author's estimates.
n.a. Not available.
a. Operational as of March 1974.
b. Less than 0.05.
c. For allies under the Military Assistance Program.
d. Includes 36 unrequested aircraft appropriated by Congress in fiscal years 1972, 1973, and 1974 at an additional cost of $528 million.
e. Approximate.
f. Includes 48 unrequested aircraft appropriated by Congress in fiscal years 1973 and 1974 at an additional cost of $170 million.

Table 3-7. Modernization Rates for Fighter and Attack Aircraft Squadrons, Fiscal Years 1962–80[a]

Average annual percentage of force reequipped

Service	1962–64	1965–68	1969–72	1973	1974	1975[b]	1976–80[b]
Air Force	10.9	14.5	4.9	7.2	0	1.6	10.2
Navy	9.1	5.7	13.6	3.0	5.8	2.8	1.8
Marine Corps	7.3	7.7	4.5	3.6	3.6	0	2.7
Overall rate	9.6	10.6	7.4	4.9	3.0	1.8	5.3

Source: Author's estimates.
a. Intraseries modernization (e.g., replacement of A-4Cs with A-4Ms or F-4Cs with F-4Es) is not considered.
b. Projected.

The F-14 undertaking has been marked by a number of program revisions. In the beginning of 1969 the plan was to acquire 463 F-14 "A" models at a total cost of $6.2 billion (in current dollars).[16] By the spring of 1971 the program had been expanded to 710 aircraft, enough to equip each of the Navy's modern attack carriers and each Marine air wing with two squadrons of F-14s. Moreover, all but the first 50-odd aircraft were to be "B" models, powered by an upgraded version of the advanced engine the Air Force plans to use in its F-15. The total cost of the new program was estimated at $8.4 billion, an increase of $2.2 billion over the original 463-aircraft program. The larger number of aircraft to be procured reduced the estimated average unit cost by $1.5 million, to $11.8 million.

Mounting cost pressures quickly led to another revision, however. In July 1971 the program was reduced to 301 aircraft, all of which would be the lower-performance "A" models equipped with a less powerful but proven engine. The estimate of total cost was set at $5.2 billion; average unit cost became $17.3 million.[17] A year later even this scaled-down program was in jeopardy because of rising costs. Professing losses at an intolerable rate on each aircraft being produced, the principal contractor for

16. Including the cost of the AWG-9 avionics system, which controls the firing of Phoenix missiles, but not the costs associated with the missile itself. The planning estimate for the total cost of the Phoenix program was $0.37 billion; the current estimate is $1.15 billion.

17. The average unit costs indicated here are several hundred thousand dollars higher than the figures stated by the Defense Department, which includes aircraft built for research and development in its computations. For example, Defense distributed the $5.2 billion total cost of the June 1971 program across 313 aircraft— 301 production aircraft and 12 research and development aircraft. Since the latter have little operational utility, they are considered here as ordinary development overhead.

the F-14 refused to deliver any aircraft beyond the 122 on order through 1973 unless the unit price was increased by $3 million.

While the Navy continued to argue the absolute necessity of acquiring F-14s, whatever the cost, disenchantment with the system began to appear in the highest echelons of the Defense Department. Deputy Secretary of Defense William P. Clements proposed to the Senate Armed Services Committee that a decision on whether to proceed with F-14A procurement be deferred until competitive trials could be held among it, an austere "D" model, a Phoenix-missile-equipped F-15 modified for carrier use, and the latest model of the F-4, and the results thoroughly appraised. This proposal was rejected on the grounds that it would be too costly and involve an excessive delay in modernizing carrier air defenses.

Compounding the Navy's difficulties in promoting the F-14, the Marine Corps, which was to have received about fifty aircraft under the July 1971 program, opted instead for an improved, more maneuverable model of the F-4—the F-4J. Testifying before the House Subcommittee on Defense Appropriations, the Marine commandant stated that the threat faced by his service was different from that faced by the Navy and cited the ability of the F-4J to satisfy Marine requirements for air support during amphibious operations as justification for the Corps's preference. This was promptly characterized by the chief of naval operations (although not by the secretary of the navy, who was also in attendance) as a "bad decision."

After a weekend of further work on the problem, the commandant returned to the hearings to reverse his earlier position that "numbers of airplanes were, if anything, more important than the improvement in quality of the F-14" (over the F-4J) by concluding that "the fighters we need are F-14s."[18] The Marine Corps, he declared, wished to apply the $890 million (the first $131 million of which was requested for 1974) it had planned to request for procuring 138 F-4Js to the F-14 program instead. In return, the Corps would receive 68 of the first 301 aircraft built (the imputed cost to the Navy of these 68 F-14As is $1.9 billion).[19] The Marine Corps would use these aircraft to form four squadrons of 12 F-14s each[20] to serve as "patrol leaders" for its F-4 squadrons and also, it was

---

18. *Department of Defense Appropriations for Fiscal Year 1974*, Hearings before a Subcommittee of the House Committee on Appropriations, 93 Cong. 1 sess. (1973), part 2, pp. 293, 294, 361, 362, 394–99.

19. See Table 4-2.

20. Existing Marine fighter squadrons equipped with F-4s have 15 aircraft apiece.

implied, assist the Navy, if requested, in defending its carriers and assault ships when these vessels were supporting Marine operations.

At present the size of the F-14A program stands at 322 production and 12 research and development aircraft, which the Defense Department now estimates will cost $6.8 billion (including, as did earlier estimates, $370 million already spent for F-14B development but not the $1.2 billion Phoenix program). If the F-14 survives its current difficulties, as now seems probable, procurement is likely to go well above this level, however. There is no precedent for buying so few aircraft of a major new design once that design has achieved operational acceptance. (Through fiscal 1974 461 tactical F-111s had been ordered for the Air Force despite the severe cost and performance problems the program encountered.) Moreover the Navy has stated that it will form twelve operational squadrons of F-14As. But the 322 aircraft in the announced program will not be enough for this many Navy squadrons and the four Marine squadrons as well.

The Defense Department has not publicly stated a requirement for further F-14s. However, as indicated in Table 3-8, if the Pentagon's estimates of training and maintenance requirements and the expected accident rate are used, a minimum of 69 additional aircraft will be needed to sustain the operating levels planned by the Navy and Marine Corps over an assumed service life of twelve years. (If the F-14 remains in service longer than that, still more aircraft would probably be needed.) Unless these levels are permitted to start shrinking virtually as they are attained, at least $1.5 billion more in F-14 procurement funds will have to be allocated starting in 1978. Procurement of Phoenix missiles for the extra aircraft will cost another $300 million, and more missiles must eventually be procured to replace those consumed in training.[21] These expenditures would sustain the announced force levels only through the mid-1980s and only under peacetime conditions.

Sharing the budget limelight with the F-14 is the Air Force's new long-range fighter, the F-15. The Air Force has announced that it plans to procure 729 F-15s, reequipping six of its existing fourteen wings of F-4s with this design by 1980. Although the F-15 program is $1.5 billion (in fiscal 1975 dollars) larger than the F-14 with Phoenix, until recently it had avoided the precipitous cost increase and consequent adverse publicity

---

21. The present Phoenix program provides only enough missiles to "reload" each operational F-14A once (2,457 missiles for 192 aircraft; 6 missiles per load).

Table 3-8. Procurement Requirements and Deficiencies in the Current F-14A Program, Navy and Marine Corps, End of Fiscal Years 1973–80
Number of aircraft

Item	1973	1974	1975	1976	1977	1978	1979	1980	Allowance for future attrition[a]	Total
Required by Navy	42	72	110	157	192	217	245	254	38	292
For operations[b]	24	48	72	96	120	132	144	144	...	...
For support[c]	18	24	38	61	72	85	101	110	...	...
Required by Marine Corps	...	...	27	42	58	75	78	81	18	99
For operations[b]	...	...	12	24	36	48	48	48	...	...
For support[c]	...	...	15	18	22	27	30	33	...	...
Cumulative number required	42	72	137	199	250	292	323	335	56	391
Cumulative number procured	122	172	222	272	322[d]	322	322	322	...	322
Procurement deficiency[e]	0	0	0	0	0	1	13	69	(56)	69

Source: Author's estimates.
a. Losses caused by accident; the average service life is assumed to be twelve years.
b. Unit equipment (UE) strength.
c. Includes aircraft required for training (25 percent of UE strength), a maintenance pipeline (18.3 percent of UE strength), and to replace operating losses, which the Navy estimates will average 4.5 percent a year—well under the rate of 6 percent or more typical of past carrier fighter aircraft.
d. Does not include 12 aircraft procured for research and development.
e. Assumes aircraft are delivered by the end of the fiscal year following the year in which they were procured.

that have attended the latter, and there seems to be little resistance to proceeding with the program the Air Force has defined.[22]

While the need for the F-14 and the F-15 has in each case been linked by its service sponsor to a specific mission (carrier air defense and long-range air superiority respectively), which has in turn set the size of the announced program (the inconsistency that has developed within the F-14 program notwithstanding), both designs embody the essential features that would enable them to replace the F-4 in all its divers roles, which include reconnaissance as well as combat missions.

Over 1,600 F-4s of various types are counted in the operational strength of the present active forces. By 1980 the basic F-4 design will be nearly a quarter of a century old, yet current modernization programs will have replaced not quite 40 percent of these aircraft: 1,000 will still be in service. Since the F-14 and the F-15 will be the only designs with comparable performance available to replace these remaining F-4s, it is highly probable that the present course will lead to much greater procurement of both types than has been specified to date by the Defense Department.

In addition, the Navy is reported to be considering the F-14 as an eventual replacement for the A-6.[23] Together, the Navy and the Marine Corps have seventeen heavy attack squadrons equipped with A-6s, and both use modified A-6s (EA-6s) for electronic warfare. Finally, the Navy must soon find a replacement for its RA-5 high-performance reconnaissance aircraft. Again, the F-14 is the most likely candidate.

Consistent with the traditional service practice of striving to maximize unit capability, the Navy and the Air Force may be expected to prefer F-14s and F-15s to any less costly designs that might be proposed for each of these applications. Thus it is important to appreciate at the outset the magnitude of the programs that would result if a policy of full modernization with F-14s and F-15s was adopted. These program potentials are summarized in Table 3-9. It should be noted that, unlike the cost estimates cited heretofore, the estimates in the table are expressed in terms of dollars of constant 1975 purchasing power.[24] For the F-14 variants it has been

22. Real (allowing for greater-than-anticipated inflation) unit acquisition cost of the F-15 has increased 31 percent for the aircraft to be procured in fiscal 1975. This follows a (nonadditive) 11 percent increase in fiscal 1974.

23. See *Aviation Week and Space Technology* (Dec. 17, 1973), p. 24.

24. The cost analysis is based on the inflation factors used by the Defense Department in preparing its 1975 budget (62 percent for research and development, 4.8 percent for procurement, and 7.6 percent for operations). To the extent that the actual rate of inflation during fiscal 1975 exceeds these allowances "constant dollar" cost estimates herein have been understated.

Table 3-9. Program Potentials for the F-14 and the F-15, Various Fiscal Years

Cost in billions of fiscal 1975 dollars

Item	Number of aircraft[a]			Cost			
	Navy	Marine Corps	Air Force	Through 1974	1975–80[b]	1981 and after	Total
F-14/Phoenix	1,000	430	...	5.8	11.7	15.7	33.2
Announced program	250	70	...	5.8	3.0	0	8.3
Procurement deficiency[c]	−40	−30	...	0	1.5	...	1.5
To replace remaining F-4s	280	120	...	0	4.8	2.7	7.5
To replace RF-4s and RA-5s	90	40	...	0	1.2	0.6	1.8
To replace A-6s	280	140	...	0	...	8.5	8.5
To replace EA-6s	60	30	...	0	...	3.9	3.9
To retrofit F-14As	(200)	(50)	...	0	1.2	...	1.2
F-15	...	...	2,000	3.1	8.8	10.3	22.2
Announced program	...	...	730	3.1	6.6	0	9.7
To replace remaining F-4s	...	...	970	0	1.4	8.1	9.5
To replace RF-4s	...	...	300	0	0.8	2.2	3.0

Source: Author's estimates.

a. Figures are rounded. They do not include aircraft that might be produced for sale to foreign nations. Iran, for example, has announced an intent to purchase 30 F-14As at a total cost of $900 million and is reported to be discussing a possible purchase of 50 to 60 F-15s costing $1 billion. Some accounts set the sales potential to Iran at 300 F-14s and 700 F-15s, or almost as many aircraft as in the announced Navy and Air Force programs (see "Washington Outlook," Business Week, Feb. 2, 1974, p. 30). Although large overseas sales would benefit the defense budget by providing economies of scale that would reduce the average cost of aircraft bought for U.S. forces, the large unit cost of the F-14 and F-15 is likely to discourage other countries from purchasing these designs except in special cases such as that of oil-rich Iran.

b. Assumes that F-14 procurement rate remains constant at 50 aircraft a year through 1977 and doubles, to 100 aircraft a year, in 1978–80. The procurement rate for the F-15 is assumed to remain constant at 144 aircraft a year in 1979 and 1980.

c. Additional aircraft needed to support announced operational levels.

assumed that all aircraft procured after fiscal 1977 would be B models and that only the aircraft used to replace Navy F-4s would be equipped with Phoenix missiles and the AWG-9 fire control system.

The dimensions of the problem to be faced if the tactical air forces are to be modernized without changing their present character or numerical strength is apparent. Even if the rate of procurement of the F-14 were to double in 1978, to 100 aircraft,[25] and remain at that $2 billion annual pace thereafter, the Navy and the Marine Corps would not acquire all the aircraft needed to modernize their fighter, heavy attack, reconnaissance, and electronic warfare forces until 1988. And by then the F-14 will be older than the F-4 is at present. The $33 billion required to complete this effort would make it the largest single-weapon acquisition program ever undertaken by the United States. Financing such a program without attendant real increases in the overall defense budget would be extremely difficult, at best.

The outlook for full Air Force modernization with the F-15 is only marginally brighter than that for the Navy with the F-14. The $22 billion it would cost to replace all the Air Force's F-4s and RF-4s with F-15s is roughly comparable to what was spent on the various facets of the Minuteman intercontinental ballistic missile program. This suggests the high priority the F-15 would have to receive to realize this program potential. If the procurement rate was maintained at 144 aircraft a year,[26] the Air Force could acquire the required number of F-15s by 1985 at an average annual cost of about $1.9 billion in fiscal 1975 dollars.

In rather sharp contrast to the F-14 and F-15, both of which embrace traditional service values, two new aircraft that can only be considered antagonistic to the doctrine of their sponsoring service, the Air Force, are being developed. Each is specialized for a particular mission and complements the other: local, or battlefield, air superiority in the case of the lightweight fighter (LWF), close air support of ground troops in the case of the A-10 (formerly A-X). Both programs were started by civilian officials in the Defense Department, have received modest funding to date, and have uncertain procurement futures.

The future of the LWF is particularly uncertain in view of the Air

25. As currently scheduled, the rate of procurement will drop from 50 aircraft a year through 1976 to 29 aircraft in 1977, ending the announced program.

26. The current schedule calls for procuring 144 aircraft each year from fiscal 1975 to 1978. The last 46 F-15s in the announced program would be procured in 1979.

Force's past lack of enthusiasm for similar high-performance but limited-payload fighters such as the F-104 and F-5, neither of which, though used extensively by U.S. allies, achieved more than nominal operating status with the Air Force. At present, the odds appear to be decidedly against any procurement of the LWF for Air Force use.[27]

For the A-10 the prospect of achieving operational status in the Air Force is somewhat better, especially if the Army and the Marine Corps continue to push competing designs for the close support mission. The Air Force position on the A-10 is that existing capabilities should not be compromised to gain the improved close air support capability it promises to provide. In other words, the A-10 should be added to the present force level, not subsumed within it.[28] The degree of enthusiasm with which the service urges procurement of the A-10 may depend on acceptance of or at least concessions on this point by the Defense Department.[29] The Air Force's doctrine of mission priorities, which is discussed at length in chapter 5, is at stake with this issue: implicit in any reequipping of existing F-4 wings with A-10s or lightweight fighters would be a shift in emphasis away from the deep penetration missions that the Air Force considers most important.

If the A-10 must be accommodated within the present force level of twenty-one wings, the Air Force has indicated that it would rather retire its three wings of A-7s than lose F-4s. A comparatively inexpensive subsonic attack aircraft derived for the Navy from an earlier fighter design, the A-7 Corsair II, has had the enthusiastic support of several influential members of Congress, who oppose its retirement, however, having successfully added funds to procure additional A-7s not requested by the Air Force in both 1973 and 1974.

Unconvinced by an Air Force cost-effectiveness study concluding that a force of 950 A-7s would be needed to provide a close support capability equivalent to that of 500 A-10s, which would cost only one-third as much to buy and operate,[30] the staunchest congressional supporters of the A-7

27. The decision to include funds in the 1975 budget for developing a new design (the air combat fighter, or ACF) following the concept of the LWF program seems consistent with this judgment.

28. *Fiscal Year 1973 Authorization for Military Procurement . . .*, Hearings before the Senate Committee on Armed Services, 92 Cong. 2 sess. (1972), pp. 3523, 3524.

29. The A-10, to be assembled on Long Island, also faces stiff political opposition in Congress from supporters of the Texas-built A-7.

30. *Nomination of McLucas and Brown,* Hearing before the Senate Committee on Armed Services, 93 Cong. 1 sess. (1973), pp. 24, 25.

continue to believe that this aircraft, not the A-10, should equip whatever additional close support wings are to be formed. As a consequence A-10 procurement, which was to have commenced last year, had to await the outcome of competitive field tests between the two designs. Since the A-10 and A-7 represent quite different approaches to carrying out the close support mission, it proved difficult to develop common criteria for comparing the aircraft on a test range. Consequently, the contest failed to produce an unequivocal "winner," although the A-10, despite its having been pitted in rough prototype form against a combat-proven model of the A-7, did achieve a slight overall advantage in the view of both Air Force pilots and civilian analysts.[31]

These considerations could still lead to the demise of the A-10. Alternatively, some or all of the A-10s might be sent directly to the Air National Guard, replacing improvised close support types in the special operating forces (SOF) squadrons that were formed for the war in Southeast Asia and subsequently placed in reserve. Though giving brand-new airplanes to the reserve forces would be highly unusual for the Air Force, it could prove to be the only workable compromise.

Procurement of a second aircraft to be used exclusively in the close support role was one of the largest tactical air programs in the 1974 budget. This is the British-built V/STOL (vertical or short-takeoff-and-landing) AV-8A Harrier, procured for the Marine Corps. Until recently a third close air support system would also have been included—the Army's AH-56 Cheyenne helicopter gunship, now canceled.[32] Both the Army and the Marine Corps argue special requirements and the unique suitability of the systems they have sponsored in meeting these requirements. The Army says that it needs an all-weather "tank-killer" for NATO defense and believes that the best solution lies in an advanced helicopter equipped with "TOW" missiles.[33] The Marine Corps argues its

31. Pilots' preference for the A-10 was based on their judgment that the A-7 could not effectively carry out the close support mission under the marginal weather conditions that prevail about 40 percent of the time in the most probable, Central European battle area. For better weather, the pilots preferred the A-7. See *Briefing by the Department of the Air Force on the Flyoff between the A-7 and A-10 Aircraft,* Hearings before the House Committee on Armed Services (H.A.S.C. 93-60), 93 Cong. 2 sess. (1974), pp. 16–50.

32. The Army has solicited design proposals for a less expensive advanced attack helicopter (AAH) in lieu of Cheyenne. For this program $59 million has been appropriated and another $61 million is requested for 1975.

33. "Tube-launched, optically guided, wire-tracked." Older helicopters equipped with these missiles proved highly effective against communist armor in the "permissive" (lightly defended) air environment over South Vietnam.

need for an aircraft that can move right along with surface elements during amphibious actions, flying first from aboard ship against beach defenses, then from the beachhead, and finally from dispersed forward sites as the assault forces move inland.[34] The Harrier program is now complete, but the Marine Corps, which has referred to the airplane as "a cogent beginning,"[35] has already begun to press for an improved follow-on to this design before the end of the decade—a new V/STOL aircraft, designated AV-16.

The principal disadvantage of the Harrier, aside from its high unit cost ($5.4 million in fiscal 1975 dollars), is its very limited range and weapons payload. In a vertical takeoff, for example, the Harrier is unable to lift the full weight of the fuel its internal tanks can hold, let alone an external munitions payload. A short takeoff run improves on this situation somewhat, and the Marine Corps believes it can make up for payload limitations by maintaining a high sortie rate (six or more a day in combat is the goal). The Harrier's maneuverability in the hands of a proficient pilot may give it an edge over the A-10 or an armed helicopter in avoiding enemy fighters, but the complexity of its flight systems may make it highly vulnerable to ground fire (a shortcoming shared by the helicopter).

The Air Force maintains that the A-10 can meet the close support needs of the land forces more effectively and at much lower cost than either the Harrier or an armed helicopter. The A-10 has very pronounced advantages in offensive punch (range and payload), and its design simplicity, armor, and redundant flight systems should make it less vulnerable to ground fire than any of its rivals. Unlike high-performance jets, which rely mostly on speed and altitude to avoid battle damage to the general detriment of the accuracy of their attack, the A-10 flying low and slowly must expect to be hit more often by ground fire, counting on its built-in durability rather than on evasive tactics to survive.[36]

34. A related problem is how well the Marines will be able to support widely dispersed Harrier operations.

35. Maj. Gen. T. H. Miller, USMC, and Lt. Col. C. M. Baker, USMC, "The AV-8A Harrier in U.S. Marine Corps Service," *International Defense Review*, vol. 6 (February 1973), pp. 61, 62.

36. Rarely can an aircraft survive a hit from a large missile, however, and the A-10 must rely on electronic countermeasures by other aircraft and its own maneuverability and low operating altitude for protection against such weapons as the SA-2, -3, and -6. The unique placement of the A-10's twin engines should afford it extra protection against low-altitude antiaircraft missiles such as the heat-seeking SA-7 Strela. Used effectively against U.S. helicopters in Southeast Asia, the SA-7 also downed a number of single-engine A-4s during the October 1973 war in the

Critics of the A-10 point to its lack of a foul-weather navigational or fire control system (a lack largely responsible for its low, $2.1 million flyaway cost[37]) as a major disadvantage. The Air Force believes that the A-10's low-altitude maneuverability will more than compensate for the absence of all-weather avionics, however, and has not urged that such equipment be installed in the A-10.[38] Nevertheless, an all-weather A-10B, at as much as twice the present model's cost, could become a reality by the end of the 1970s.

Another aircraft under development with major program potential during the 1970s is the advanced medium short-takeoff-and-landing transport (AMST), for which $56 million for research and development in fiscal 1975 has been requested. The AMST is intended eventually to replace the highly successful C-130 for the tactical airlift mission. Again, the main debate concerns which kind of aircraft would be most useful. As with close air support, the Army is the principal consumer of a service that the Air Force is responsible for providing. There have been indications that the Army would prefer a somewhat smaller aircraft optimized for a purely tactical role—a modern replacement for the aging and dwindling fleet of C-7s (a type that was under Army control until 1968) and C-123s to fill what it feels to be a gap between its own heavy-lift helicopters and the big four-engined C-130.[39]

Once again, the Air Force preference is for a larger, more versatile design with a multimission capability and longer range. Though described by the Air Force as a tactical transport, the range and payload capabilities of the AMST, like those of the C-130, will permit intermediate-range quasi-strategic airlift missions as well. Achieving more capability at the upper end of the airlift mission spectrum inevitably means a sacrifice at the lower end, however, with the requirements for speed, range, and pay-

Middle East, although many such types reportedly managed to survive SA-7 hits. See "Israeli Air Force: Decisive in War," *Aviation Week and Space Technology* (Dec. 3, 1973), p. 18.

37. Flyaway cost is the full production cost of the complete aircraft but does not include spare parts, specialized support equipment, or the costs of research and development. The total cost of a 729-aircraft A-10 program was revised upward by $221 million in August 1973 to $2.49 billion (in current dollars). Much of the increase is attributable to greater than anticipated inflation and the delay imposed by congressional demands that the A-10 prove its superiority over the A-7.

38. In any event the all-weather fire control systems on existing aircraft are not sufficiently advanced to provide the precision needed for close support operations under the most extreme weather conditions.

39. The last remaining squadrons of C-7s and C-123s are now in reserve status.

load detracting from the AMST's ability to operate in and out of forward areas, and its higher cost limiting the occasions when its commitment to high-risk resupply flights can be justified.[40] Over 1,000 AMSTs would be needed to reequip all seventeen active and twenty-nine reserve squadrons of C-130s, and this would cost $6 billion to $8 billion, most of which would probably be spent in the 1980s. At least one of the two designs being developed under the AMST program could have a profitable future in the commercial market as well.[41]

Rounding out the list of the top new tactical air programs are the E-3A Advanced Warning and Control System (AWACS), a Boeing model 707 airplane outfitted with extensive radar and communications equipment to permit it to manage both tactical and strategic defensive counterair operations; the AIM-7F Sparrow radar-guided air-to-air missile, which, if successful, is intended gradually to replace earlier models of the same series; and the AGM-53 Condor air-to-surface missile designed to outrange existing defensive antiair missiles. Research and development funds are also requested for work on an electronic warfare version of the F-111 fighter-bomber. Although no procurement program for this EF-111 has yet been defined, conversion of one wing of existing F-111s would cost about $1 billion.

Operations

Each year most of the public attention and congressional scrutiny directed at the defense budget focuses on the funds requested to acquire new military hardware. Although spending for major weapon systems accounts for less than one-fourth the total cost of maintaining the present tactical air forces, this attention is both understandable, spending for weaponry being not only the most visible part of the defense budget but also the part most amenable to year-by-year management, and well founded because of the extremely rapid growth in weapons costs and the pertinence of decisions about them in determining future costs in other sectors of the defense budget.

40. The Air Force's target price for the AMST is reportedly $5 million in fiscal 1973 dollars. This will present a real challenge for the aviation industry if it is also to produce a design markedly superior to the C-130, which cost $4.5 million apiece to procure in 1973.

41. Development of the first pure-jet U.S. airliner, the widely accepted Boeing 707, benefited substantially from the Air Force KC-135 aerial tanker program during the 1950s.

In the short term operating costs, largely in the form of pay and allowances for military and civilian personnel and procurement of consumables such as petroleum products, are dependent primarily on the size of the forces. Over the longer term the composition of the forces as reflected in the kinds of major weapons with which they are equipped is also important. To the extent that modernization leads to more complex weapons, it usually also means weapons that are more costly to operate and to maintain. This consideration had a particularly acute effect on operating costs during the 1960s, when the new aircraft that came into service, such as the F-105, the F-4, and the F-111, were much more expensive to keep in the air than the types they replaced. In one hour of flying time, for example, an F-4 or F-105 burns 40 percent more fuel than an F-100 ($490 for the F-4 and the F-105 as against $350 for the F-100).[42]

Servicing costs also increased sharply with the new aircraft introduced in the 1960s, which typically require better than thirty man-hours of ground maintenance for each hour of flight whereas the design generation they replaced required twenty or less. Increasing size, sophistication, and complexity have also worked to raise operating costs in more subtle ways: training costs for skilled technicians, carrying charges for parts inventories, and more elaborate servicing equipment, to cite a few.

A growing awareness of this problem has led designers to give more attention to serviceability, which may temper somewhat, if not arrest entirely, the upward trend in flying-hour costs. It is not known for certain what the F-14 or F-15 will cost to operate, but neither should be much more costly than the already expensive F-4; and real savings should be produced as A-7 (or possibly F-4) squadrons are converted to the A-10, the amount depending on the rate of conversion.[43] Further savings will result from the expected reduction in Navy fighter and attack squadrons. Together, these considerations should largely offset any marginal cost increases attendant on the introduction of the F-14, the F-15, and the AMST, although only a limited number of the latter could become opera-

42. *Department of Defense Appropriations for 1973*, Hearings before the Senate Committee on Appropriations, 92 Cong. 2 sess. (1972), part 4, p. 307. The costs cited in the Hearings are expressed in fiscal 1972 dollars and have been adjusted to reflect the price increases in jet aviation fuel, which in 1972 sold for 11 cents a gallon but now sells for 35 cents a gallon. Increased fuel prices will inflate the 1975 operating budget for the tactical air forces by an estimated $500 million to $700 million over that for 1974.

43. Preliminary estimates for the A-10 suggest that fewer than ten man-hours of ground maintenance will be needed to support one flying hour. The A-7 requires twenty-five maintenance man-hours per flying hour; the F-4 more than thirty.

Table 3-10. Cost of Baseline Tactical Air Forces, Fiscal Years 1974–80
Billions of fiscal 1975 dollars

Type of cost	Actual, 1974	Requested, 1975[a]	Projected					1975–80	
			1976	1977	1978	1979	1980	Total	Average
Investment	9.1	9.9	9.2	8.7	9.0	10.3	10.6	57.7	9.6
Major systems	5.1	5.0	4.6	4.2	4.6	5.9	6.1	30.4	5.1
Other	4.0	4.9	4.6	4.5	4.4	4.4	4.5	27.3	4.5
Operations	13.6	13.7	13.9	13.9	14.0	13.9	14.0	83.4	13.9
Active forces	5.8	6.0	6.1	6.1	6.1	6.0	6.0	36.3	6.1
Reserve forces	1.2	1.2	1.3	1.3	1.4	1.4	1.5	8.1	1.4
Indirect support[b]	6.6	6.5	6.5	6.5	6.5	6.5	6.5	39.0	6.5
Total	22.7	23.6	23.1	22.6	23.0	24.2	24.6	141.1	23.5

Source: Author's estimates.
a. Includes concurrent supplemental request.
b. Operating costs incurred in Programs 3 (intelligence and communications), 7 (central supply and maintenance), 8 (training, medical, and other general personnel activities), and 9 (administration and associated activities), allocated in proportion to the direct operating costs of the various mission forces.

tional before 1980. Certainly there appears to be little likelihood that modernization will generate as much pressure on real operating costs for the active forces in the 1970s as was experienced in the 1960s (although inflationary pressure on consumables such as petroleum products may be particularly severe).

As new aircraft enter the active duty forces or as the size of the active forces is reduced, the older aircraft displaced in the process are rarely scrapped. Instead they are delivered to the reserve forces where they in turn "bump" still older types. Under the present program with its roughly constant active force levels, the pace of modernization in the reserves will be almost entirely dependent on the rate at which new aircraft types enter the active forces. Because major new weapons are seldom procured explicitly for the reserves, reserve costs are essentially operating costs.

The reserves have already received a few squadrons of the expensive-to-operate types of aircraft that pushed operating costs up so sharply for the active forces in the 1960s, and they have begun to feel the same sort of cost pressures, compounded by the worn state of these aircraft. This trend will continue and perhaps intensify somewhat between 1976 and 1980 as the influx of F-4s displaced from the active forces by F-14s and F-15s gains momentum.

Costs

The cost of supporting baseline tactical air forces is projected through 1980 in Table 3-10. The estimates include the costs of procuring and operating the Navy's attack aircraft carriers and all the tactical elements of Air Force, Navy, and Marine Corps active and reserve air units. Not included are costs associated with the escort and auxiliary ships that support the Navy's carrier task forces, or the Army's attack helicopters and tactical air defense units. "Indirect support" costs include myriad activities (intelligence, communications, general personnel and administration) that cannot be readily tied to specific mission forces.

It should be stressed that the estimates shown are based on the author's interpretation of the likely course of present policy, which is not, of course, a certain path. The problem of adequately allowing for programs not yet defined, or perhaps even conceived, tends to depress long-range forecasts of this sort and may lead to an understatement of the costs actually incurred during the last portion of the projection period.

Table 3-11. Distribution of Tactical Air Costs, Fiscal Years 1974–80

Billions of fiscal 1975 dollars

Service	Actual, 1974	Requested, 1975[a]	Projected					1975–80	
			1976	1977	1978	1979	1980	Total	Average[b]
Air Force	12.8	14.0	13.5	13.2	13.8	13.9	14.2	82.6	13.8
Navy[c]	7.3	6.9	7.0	6.9	6.8	7.7	7.8	43.1	7.2
Marine Corps[d]	2.6	2.7	2.6	2.5	2.4	2.6	2.6	15.4	2.6
Total	22.7	23.6	23.1	22.6	23.0	24.2	24.6	141.1	23.5

Source: Author's estimates.

a. Includes concurrent supplemental request.

b. Figures are rounded.

c. Includes costs associated with aircraft carriers as well as carrier air wings, but does not include costs associated with escort and auxiliary vessels required to protect and supply the carriers.

d. With the exception of the cost of the military personnel (including the reserves), which is estimated for 1975 as $417 million, all direct costs associated with supporting Marine tactical air forces are part of the Navy budget.

Overall investment in major weapon systems is down slightly in 1975. The 1974 total of $5.1 billion included $690 million to complete the funding of a new aircraft carrier, CVN-70, however. No money is requested for carrier construction in 1975. Investment in aircraft and missile systems will be $0.6 billion higher this year than last. Other investment is also up sharply, primarily as a result of the current effort to improve the readiness of the forces. Investment costs are projected to dip slightly in the next three years but to climb to $1 billion above the current level by the end of the decade. No appreciable increases in operating costs are anticipated, although reserve costs may be expected to increase by at least 25 percent, to an annual pace of $1.5 billion (in fiscal 1975 dollars). Overall costs are expected to average close to the 1975 level of $23.6 billion.

As shown in Table 3-11, the Air Force received slightly more than one-half the money appropriated for the tactical air forces last year, and it should continue to receive about the same portion throughout the forecast period unless the decision is made to commence full modernization of Navy and Marine air wings with the F-14. The table shows the actual and projected distribution of funds among the three services.

CHAPTER FOUR

THE COST EVOLUTION OF
U.S. TACTICAL WARPLANES

The positive side of technological substitution—lower casualty rates and a more efficient military—and the importance of tactical air power in realizing these benefits have been discussed. The major programs for acquiring new weapon systems for the tactical air forces were described and projections made about how the size and complexion of these forces are likely to evolve in the 1970s under present policy. The most prominent feature of these projections is the huge cost of acquiring a relatively small number of F-14s and F-15s. This calls attention to the negative side of technological substitution—the high level to which the costs of some weapons have risen.

The means of sustaining the man-to-machines trend in the future must come from the same source as in the past: ever more efficacious weapons. Usually greater weapon performance has meant greater weapon complexity, and greater complexity has meant greater unit costs.[1] While neither the phenomenon of rapidly rising equipment costs nor the hard choices regarding mission priorities and the quantity-quality trade-off they impose are new (the analysis that follows demonstrates a remarkably consistent pattern for U.S. tactical warplane designs over the last thirty years), it may well be that a threshold of intolerance is about to be reached. That is, the cumulative pressure generated by thirty years of mounting unit costs may be approaching the point where many systems designed and built to traditional U.S. standards of versatility and ultra-sophistication will be too expensive to be bought in significant quantities.

Rising Unit Costs

U.S. tactical air power is perhaps the purest example of applied military technology within the general purpose forces, and nowhere is the problem

---

1. But not always. Improved performance does not necessarily entail more complex and more costly systems; this is a matter of choice.

of how to sustain the benefits from technological substitution in the face of exploding unit costs more evident. The extent of the problem is easily illustrated. During the peak procurement year of World War II (1943) the Army Air Corps committed $2.47 billion to purchase tactical aircraft: fighters and light and medium bombers of a dozen popular types. For fiscal year 1975 the Air Force requested $1.07 billion to buy modern airplanes for the same tactical purposes. The difference is that in 1943 the Army got 24,847 airplanes for its money; this year the Air Force wants to buy 98. The average cost of a tactical warplane procured in 1943 was $99,400. In 1975 it will be $10,900,000.[2]

Few other classes of military hardware come close to matching this multiple of cost growth. The most expensive tactical aircraft now being procured, the Navy's F-14 Tomcat, is 190 times as costly as its World War II kin, the F4U Corsair. By comparison, the latest nuclear-powered aircraft carrier, CVN-70, though the focus of much public attention in fiscal 1974 because of its billion-dollar price tag, is only 18 times as expensive as the Essex class of World War II carriers.[3] Even the controversial battle tank, MBT-70, an austere version of which (XM-803) was still rejected as too expensive by Congress, would have been priced at no more than 15 times the cost of the most widely used U.S. battle tank of World War II, the $55,000 M-4 Sherman.

Compared to other kinds of aircraft, the climb in unit costs for tactical warplanes appears less extraordinary, though even in this company the tactical air curve remains prominent, exceeded only by the growth for strategic bombers. (The B-1, if produced, will probably be at least 200 times as expensive as the heaviest bombers of World War II.) At a fly-away cost on the order of $20 million, the Boeing model 747 is nearly 70 times as expensive as the most advanced commercial airliner in service immediately after the war, the Douglas DC-4. The Air Force's C-5A, with all the difficulties it has encountered, costs 130 times as much as the military version of the DC-4, the C-54.

Whatever one's position on the value of tactical air power, its appropriate claim on the finite resources available for national defense, or the

2. U.S. Department of Defense, "Program Acquisition Costs by Weapon System: Department of Defense Budget for Fiscal Year 1974" (1973; processed), pp. 19, 21, 24. Irving Brinton Holley, Jr., *Buying Aircraft: Materiel Procurement for the Army Air Forces*, Office of the Chief of Military History, Department of the Army (1964), pp. 558, 560. This does not include aircraft purchased for allies.

3. *CVAN-70 Aircraft Carrier*, Hearings before the Joint Subcommittee of the Senate and House Armed Services Committees, 91 Cong. 2 sess. (1970), pp. 110–12.

mission capabilities it should seek to achieve, the upward trend in the unit cost of tactical aircraft and where it may be leading can only be cause for concern. Rather than accept the risk of an abrupt confrontation a few years hence with a generation of aircraft that have priced themselves out of the weapons market, as did the Army's MBT-70, it seems wise to face the issue of unit costs squarely now by trying to identify what factors have caused the steep climb and by considering means of breaking free of the spiral.

To do this, it is useful to establish the historical cost trend in more definite terms. First, however, allowance must be made for the most obvious factor at work: inflation. That is, one must distinguish between changes in the "price" of tactical warplanes as measured in "current dollars" and changes in their "real cost" as measured in dollars of "constant purchasing power." Conversion factors (price deflators) specifically applicable to military aircraft are not available. However, a reasonable approximation may be found in the statistics maintained by the Department of Commerce on federal purchases of goods and services in general.[4]

According to these data, the cumulative effect of inflation has reduced the quantity of resources measured by a 1975 dollar to about one-fourth of the quantity measured by a dollar in 1940.[5] In the analysis that follows, unless otherwise noted, all costs are stated in dollars of constant fiscal 1975 purchasing power.

The Trend in Fighter Costs

The modern U.S. high-performance fighter is a hybrid. Part of its heritage is the smallish bomber that flourished briefly during World War II, but a larger part can be traced to the fighter (formerly "pursuit") types of that era. At the outset of World War II the mainstay of the Army's fighter forces was the Curtiss P-40. Immortalized by the grinning shark jaws emblazoned on the planes of the Flying Tigers, the P-40 was a new design somewhat larger and heavier than the standard fighters used by the Germans and the Japanese. Mass production brought the average flyaway cost of the P-40 down to $200,000 (in 1975 dollars). The P-40's performance proved generally inferior to the planes it met in combat, how-

4. Corrected for the disproportionately large real wage increases granted to federal employees in recent years.

5. *Economic Report of the President, January 1973,* p. 197.

ever, and its range was inadequate for many missions, so U.S. production was quickly switched to more highly powered, longer-range types.

Land-based fighter production during the last two years of the war concentrated on two aircraft, the P-47 Thunderbolt and the P-51 Mustang. Both represented an increase in size and range over the most popular early war designs, and at $310,000 each the P-47 was half again as costly to produce as the P-40. Performance was vastly improved with both aircraft, however, and the advantage in aerial combat shifted abruptly to American pilots flying these types. In the P-47, the P-51, and their Navy contemporary the F4U, all proficient at attacking ground targets as well as flying long distances to engage enemy fighters in aerial combat, can be found the genesis of the multipurpose design philosophy that has, with only an occasional lapse, dominated U.S. military thinking since.

The design preferences that emerged from World War II became more firmly set in Korea, where the F-86 Sabre was pitted against the Soviet-built MIG-15 in large-scale air battles deep over hostile territory. Once again, the American design was the bigger, more complex aircraft, and its cost ($710,000) equaled that of the most expensive warplane in the U.S. arsenal ten years earlier (the four-engined B-24 Liberator heavy bomber). Nevertheless, the F-86 system, including the better-trained American pilot,[6] was clearly cost-effective against the MIG-15 as evidenced by the remarkable kill ratio it achieved over the Soviet-designed jet under tactical conditions that greatly favored the communist side.[7]

The success of the F-86 in Korea seems to have dispelled whatever doubt U.S. planners may still have had about the qualities that should be built into tactical aircraft. Throughout the remainder of the 1950s, new designs proliferated. Aside from the specialized attack aircraft that endured in the Navy, the designs that gained widespread operational status became successively bigger, more versatile, more complex, and more costly than their predecessors, culminating toward the end of the decade in the development of the F-4 Phantom II.

Originally intended to serve the Navy and the Marine Corps in an attack role, the F-4 was redesignated a fighter early in its development and

---

6. The question of the relative importance of different facets of aircraft performance, armament, and aircrew proficiency in air battles is a matter of continuing discussion, as is the military utility of protracted day-in-day-out dogfights of the "MIG Alley" variety carried out in relative isolation from the land battle.

7. "USAF Tactical Operations, World War II and Korean War" (USAF Historical Division, 1962; processed), pp. 165, 166.

charged with the primary mission of fleet air defense. When the Air Force adopted the design to augment its own F-105s for long-range tactical strikes, including delivery of nuclear weapons, the F-4 became the first, and so far only, combat aircraft to achieve acceptance by the three services.[8] Early versions of the F-4 cost about $3.8 million each. The latest models, which incorporate many improvements in aerodynamics, engines, and avionics, cost nearly $6 million.

The latest tactical warplane for which certain cost data exist is the F-111. The technical difficulties encountered with this highly innovative system and the way in which these problems raised the design's cost and delayed its operational contribution are well known. While the Air Force holds that the refined F-111 has become a successful long-range attack aircraft, its capabilities in aerial combat remain something of a disappointment.

Table 4-1 summarizes some of the vital statistics for twelve of the U.S. fighters most widely used since 1940 and for the now emerging F-14 and F-15. Figure 4-1 shows the cost evolution graphically by plotting the average flyaway cost of each design against the year in which the design first became operational. (Current cost estimates for the lightweight fighter are included so that this concept can be compared with traditional designs.) Over the twenty-seven years separating the F-111 and the P-40, the real cost of producing a single first-line fighter increased eightyfold.[9] What factors have been responsible for this trend?

One reason frequently cited is the loss of production economies of scale. Instead of building ten or fifteen thousand airplanes of the same basic design using assembly line methods as in the 1940s, production runs are now measured in hundreds[10] and the aircraft are largely handcrafted. Analysis of World War II production data indicates that, as the number built rose, average costs declined roughly as shown in Figure 4-2.

If the same principles that dictated production costs in the 1940s remained applicable for modern designs (which may, however, be some-

8. The Navy-developed A-7 is also used extensively by the Air Force though not by the Marine Corps, which retains the A-4 for light attack duties.

9. Inclusion of research and development costs, which not only are much greater for modern designs but also must be allocated across fewer production units, would further increase the upward slope of the cost trend.

10. The notable exception being the F-4. The exceptionally large number of aircraft of this type built is attributable to several factors: its widespread use in many roles, losses in Southeast Asia, and the unusual (for the United States) duration of its production run.

Table 4-1. The Evolution of U.S. Fighter Aircraft

Aircraft	Year first operational	Average flyaway cost[a] (thousands)			Number built[c]	Weight (thousands of pounds)	
		Current dollars	Deflator[b]	Fiscal 1975 dollars		Empty	Gross
P-40	1940	54	27.6	200	13,738	6	8
P-51	1942	54	29.0	190	14,686	7	12
P-47	1943	91	29.4	310	15,682	10	18
F4U	1944	102	29.2	350	12,571	9	15
F9F	1949	280	39.7	710	1,078	9	16
F-86	1950	299	39.6	760	6,227	11	18
F-84F	1954	466	45.4	1,000	2,711	12	27
F-100	1955	741	47.4	1,600	2,294	21	35
F8U	1957	1,100	52.6	2,100	1,073	17	29
F-105	1958	2,500	54.5	4,600	833	28	52
F-4[d]	1961	2,200	57.2	3,800	4,600	28	54
F-111[d]	1967	10,200	66.2	15,400	449	42	77
F-14A[d, e]	1973[f]	16,000	93.9	17,000	322	37	57
F-15[d, e]	1975[f]	9,800	106.4	9,200	729	28	52[g]

Sources: *CVAN-70 Aircraft Carrier*, Hearings before the Joint Subcommittee of the Senate and House Armed Services Committees, 91 Cong. 2 sess. (1970), p. 111; Irving Brinton Holley, Jr., *Buying Aircraft: Materiel Procurement for the Army Air Forces*, Office of the Chief of Military History, Department of the Army (1964), pp. 550–60; *Economic Report of the President, January 1972*, p. 199; John W. R. Taylor and Gordon Swanborough, *Military Aircraft of the World* (Scribner's, 1971), pp. 57, 94, 106, 107, 112, 113, 138, 174, 188; *Jane's All the World's Aircraft* (London: Jane's Yearbooks, various years); *Bomber Defense of the Continental United States and Tactical Air Defense*, Hearings before the Senate Armed Services Committee, 92 Cong. 1 sess. (1971), part 5, p. 3799; Hearings before the Senate Appropriations Committee, 92 Cong. 1 sess. (1971), part 3, *Department of the Navy*, p. 1132, and part 4, *Department of the Air Force*, p. 31; "Review of F-14 Fighter Costs," Report to the Joint Economic Committee by the Comptroller General (Sept. 3, 1971; processed), enclosure 5; "U.S. Military Aircraft," *Aviation Week and Space Technology*, March 11, 1974; William Green and Gerald Pollinger, *The Aircraft of the World* (Doubleday, 1965).

a. Procurement cost of complete aircraft including airframe, engines, and avionics. Does not include cost of research and development, spare parts, or associated support equipment and facilities. The estimate for the F-14A includes the cost of a full combat load of six Phoenix missiles.

b. Fiscal year 1975 = 100.

c. Excludes foreign production.

d. Design still being produced. "Number built" is the number of aircraft in the announced procurement program as of March 1974.

e. Estimated.

f. Target date.

g. Maximum range configuration. Gross weight exclusive of externally mounted fuel or munitions is approximately 41,000 pounds.

what less susceptible to mass production techniques), the average cost of an F-14 could be reduced by nearly one-third if it were produced in the same quantity as was the F4U during World War II. To build the additional 12,237 F-14s needed to match F4U production would still cost $170 billion, however, or nearly twice as much as the entire defense budget for 1975. The argument that modern fighters seem more costly than they really are because of the penalties imposed by uneconomic pro-

Figure 4-1. Trend in Unit Cost of U.S. Fighter Designs[a]

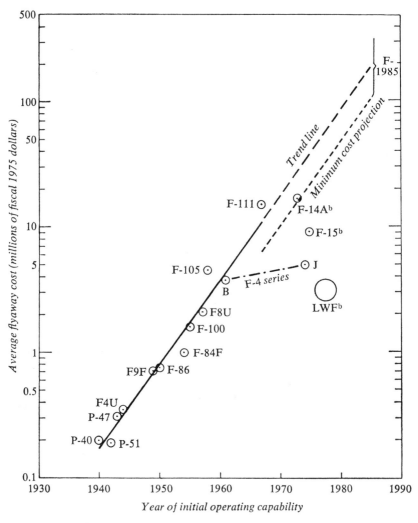

Year of initial operating capability

Sources: Same as Table 4-1.

a. Costs are plotted on a semilogarithmic scale to facilitate discrimination among the earlier aircraft. A trend line for 1940–67 is fitted by the method of least squares. This line is projected through 1980 along with the minimum cost associated with it at a statistical level of confidence of 95 percent.

b. Estimated.

duction runs therefore confuses cause and effect. It is not so much that modern aircraft are so costly because fewer are built as it is that fewer are built because modern aircraft are so costly. Through the constraint of total costs, production of fewer aircraft becomes the pragmatic corollary to

Figure 4-2. Average Unit Cost of World War II Aircraft in Relation to Number Produced[a]

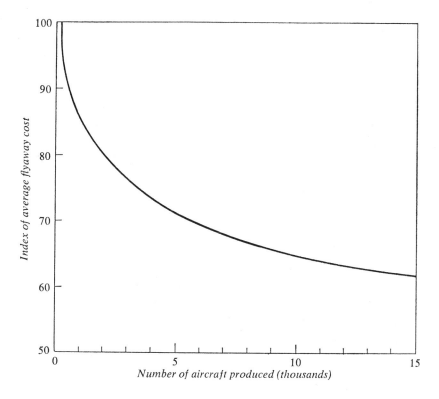

a. Variation of 5 percent, plus or minus, from the average relation reflected by the curve was typical of specific World War II designs.

expensive aircraft designs. The effects of lower production must be viewed as a secondary, dependent factor in the cost trend.

This leaves increasing technical complexity, manifest both in the growing size of the aircraft and in the ever-greater precision and sophistication of their component parts, as the principal explanation for the upward trend in unit costs. But need costs have risen so sharply? The answer, of course, is no. The rise is the product of a particular strategy to which the United States has adhered in developing new fighters, a strategy probably best characterized as one of maximizing unit capability.[11] Reflecting this

11. Rear Admiral T. R. McClellan, Chief of the Navy's Air Systems Command, put it succinctly in a response to a question from Senator Stuart Symington as to why Grumman's design for the F-14, though more expensive, was selected over one submitted by McDonnell Douglas: "In a fighter aircraft, sir, we try to get the maxi-

preference, all the designs considered here share two basic traits. First, each has been versatile; that is, each has had the capability, insofar as the technology of its day would permit, to carry out several distinctly different combat missions.[12] Second, each was designed very close to the limits of technological feasibility. Together, these qualities form the essence of the traditional U.S. design philosophy. Nothing inherent in this approach allows it to be unequivocally labeled right or wrong. The important thing is to recognize that it is only one of several strategies that could be used to exploit technological progress.

The F-14, the F-15, and the "F-1985"

Since the first F-4s entered service for the Navy in 1961, this design series has been produced in greater number than any other modern U.S. warplane, but the Navy, the Marine Corps, and the Air Force will shortly begin replacing this workhorse with new F-14s and F-15s. Under the programs set out by the Defense Department, the average cost of acquiring 322 F-14s with Phoenix missiles for the Navy and Marine Corps will be $28.1 million and the cost of 729 Air Force F-15s will average $13.4 million. A breakdown of these estimates is shown in Table 4-2.

Many who scrutinize defense spending view the high costs of the F-14 and the F-15 with dismay, if not outrage. Placed in a historical perspective, however, the unit cost of each is surprising only in being lower than might have been expected, significantly lower in the case of the F-15.[13] Table 4-3 compares the current estimates of the cost of each design with the estimates that result from projecting the cost trend established by their predecessors from 1940 to 1967. Based on the past pattern of cost growth, a new fighter design introduced in fiscal 1973, the year in which the F-14 was scheduled to join the fleet, would be expected to have a flyaway cost

---

mum design we can get." *Bomber Defense, Tactical Airpower and the F-14,* Hearings before the Senate Armed Services Committee, 92 Cong. 2 sess. (1973), part 6, p. 3788.

12. One must acknowledge slight distinctions in this generalization. Some designs, such as the P-47, F4U, F-100, and F-4 were truly multimission types. Others proved more adept at a particular mission: air combat for the F-86 and F8U, long-range attack for the F-105 and F-111.

13. Although lower than would be expected from a projection of the historical cost trend, the cost of the F-14A is not enough lower to meet the strict test of statistical significance.

Table 4-2. Estimated Average Unit Cost of the F-14A and the F-15
Millions of fiscal 1975 dollars[a]

Cost	F-14A			F-15 aircraft
	Aircraft	Phoenix	Total	
Flyaway	14.8	2.2	17.0	9.2
Spares and support	2.4	1.1	3.5	1.1
Prorated research and development	4.4[b]	3.2[c]	7.6	3.1
Total weapon acquisition cost	21.6	6.5	28.1	13.4

Sources: Senate Appropriations Committee Hearings for Fiscal Year 1974, 93 Cong. 1 sess. (1973), part 3, *Department of the Navy*, pp. 1291; Department of Defense Budget for Fiscal Year 1975, *Program Acquisition Costs by Weapon System*, pp. 8, 24; Senate Appropriations Committee Hearings for Fiscal Year 1973, 92 Cong. 2 sess. (1972), part 4, *Department of the Air Force*, p. 481.

a. Based on procurement of 322 F-14s and 729 F-15s. Average weapon acquisition cost in current dollars, assuming 4.5 percent annual inflation beyond fiscal 1975, is estimated at $23.9 million for the F-14A with Phoenix and $13.7 million for the F-15.

b. Estimate does not include $371 million spent on research and development for F-14B engine through fiscal 1974.

c. Estimate includes $500 million spent in the 1960s on a stand-off missile similar to Phoenix that was to be carried by the F-110 and later by the F-111B. Technology gained from this was transferred to Phoenix.

of $31.5 million, or nearly twice what the latest public estimate says the F-14 will cost. For a new design introduced in 1975, the year in which plans called for the F-15 to become operational, the flyaway cost might have been expected to be four and a half times the Defense Department's current estimate for the F-15. Moreover, at $9.2 million, the current estimated flyaway cost of the F-15 is less than half the minimum cost estimate, which is statistically consistent with the 1940–67 trend.

There are two possible explanations for the F-15's divergence from the cost trend of the past thirty years. Either the current estimate is grossly in error, or the aircraft is in fact the first major new U.S. fighter design in three decades to depart significantly from the cost spiral produced by the American tradition of maximizing unit capability.

The 1975 budget reveals a 31 percent increase in the unit procurement cost of the F-15 besides the extra money needed to compensate for the greater than anticipated rate of inflation.[14] Since the aircraft is not yet in

14. During congressional hearings on the 1973 defense budget, the Air Force estimated that it would require $196 million in research and development funding for the F-15 in fiscal year 1974 and $435 million for a planned procurement of 77 aircraft that year; and $47 million for R&D and $1.28 billion for procuring 144 aircraft in 1975. Actual obligations in 1974 were $258 million for R&D and $871 million to procure 62 aircraft. This year, another $183 million has been requested for R&D and $893 million to procure 72 aircraft (only half as many as previously planned). Aside from inflation, part of the increase in R&D costs may be attributed to lessened Navy participation in the joint F-15/F-14B engine development pro-

Table 4-3. Current Estimates of F-14A and F-15 Costs Compared with Trend Projection Costs
Fiscal 1975 dollars

	F-14A[a]		F-15	
Item	*Average flyaway cost (millions)*	*Total program cost (billions)*	*Average flyaway cost (millions)*	*Total program cost (billions)*
Current estimate	17.0	9.0	9.2	9.7
Trend projection				
Expected	31.5	14.0	43.6	37.4
Minimum	14.5	7.8	23.7	21.3

Source: Author's estimates.
a. Includes costs associated with AIM-54A (Phoenix) missile system, but does not include costs associated with the development of the F-401 engine being considered for F-14B.

operational status, ample time remains for real cost to rise still further. There is little risk in assuming that the cost pressures on the F-15 program are immense and that some additional real cost increases are virtually certain. It seems most unlikely, however, that F-15 flyaway costs will climb sufficiently to meet the criterion for statistical consistency with the historical trend. To do so, the present estimate would have to increase by a factor of 2.6.

If the present estimate is not this much in error, what else might account for the F-15's comparatively low price tag? Part of the answer lies with the estimating base. Whereas the estimate for the F-14 system is properly comprehensive, including all costs associated with its primary armament—the Phoenix missile—the F-15 estimate does not encompass armament costs. The justification for this exclusion is that the armament the F-15 will carry, which for counterair duties will include a new 25-mm Gatling gun and a combination of Sidewinder and advanced Sparrow missiles, has not been developed solely for use by the F-15, as the Phoenix has been for the F-14, but will be used by other fighters as well. In any event, adding in the cost of a full load of armament, though this would increase the flyaway cost of the F-15 system by upwards of $1 million,[15] still leaves the F-15 only half as costly as the F-14.

---

gram, but probably costs have risen elsewhere as well. In the procurement account, part of the cost increase is attributed to the slowdown in the procurement rate. However, it is likely that rising costs are responsible for the slower procurement rate rather than the other way around.

15. Production costs of the Sparrow "F" missile have averaged around $150,000; the F-15 will carry four plus the other weapons mentioned.

Another factor that appears to be holding down F-15 costs is the importance placed on "producibility" during the design phase of the aircraft's development. This early attention may cut assembly time and costs below the levels customarily associated with high-performance aircraft. In a similar vein, the larger number of aircraft in the F-15 program also serves to lower average unit costs, both by providing a larger base over which to distribute the fixed costs of production and by making use of the more efficient assembly methods that evolve with experience and repetition.

While each of these considerations works to narrow the gap between what it is said the F-15 will cost and what it would be expected to cost as the latest progeny of the U.S. design tradition, taken together they fall well short of explaining the full difference. Is the F-15 design divergent in some other, fundamental way from the family of fighters on which the cost trend is based?

Although the Air Force has consistently emphasized an air combat role for the F-15, just as the Navy has stressed the F-14's specific capability to guard the airspace over the fleet, in neither case will the design's utility be limited to the specified task. Both aircraft have the basic range and performance traits and the structural provisions required to deliver large payloads against ground targets deep inside hostile territory and could be readily adapted to missions of this kind. In versatility, or multimission capability, each aircraft thus conforms to the tradition for U.S. fighter designs.

The Navy's F-14 also seems to conform to the second tenet of the American design tradition in pressing the limits of existing technological feasibility, as earlier designs did. For the F-15, however, technological restraint is evident in some design areas. This is most apparent in the airframe, which does not have the variable geometry wing (pioneered in the F-111 and incorporated in the F-14) and makes no provision in the operational model for a second crewman,[16] and in the avionics which, compared to the F-14 with its $2.5 million fire control system, might be described as conservative.[17] Much less so are the aircraft's engines, the area in which the greatest technical risks were assumed and which seems to pose the greatest threat of serious cost growth.

In a general sense the quest for ever-greater top speed and ceiling, con-

16. The Air Force customarily mans fighters with a single pilot. Every seventh F-15 will, however, be a two-seater to allow it to be used for training.

17. This is not to imply that the F-15 is an unsophisticated aircraft, only that it is less complex in several ways than the F-14. Compared to Soviet designs, both of the American fighters are extremely sophisticated.

siderably overrated performance attributes in most situations, appears to have been deemphasized somewhat in the design specifications for the F-15—leading to some expressions of skepticism from Congress about the adequacy of the aircraft against emerging Soviet designs. Perhaps the most tangible indicator of cost-motivated restraint in the F-15 is the aircraft's weight. Although by no means a small airplane by international standards, the F-15 does not follow the weight-growth pattern typical of earlier generations of U.S. fighters. At an "empty" weight of 28,000 pounds, the F-15 is no heavier than the F-4 it will replace, and it is about ten tons lighter than the F-111—the heaviest fighter ever produced.

Scale alone fails to fully reflect technical complexity, however. Further insight can be gained by examining the production cost per unit of weight of a design. During World War II an average cost of $20 to $30 a pound was the rule for U.S. fighters. The F-15 will cost $330 a pound, two and one-half times the cost of the F-4 but no more than the F-111 and nearly one-third less than the F-14 with its costly avionics.

The extent to which the F-15 succumbs to further cost growth could hold ominous connotations for the future of manned tactical warplanes, or at least those built to the American tradition described in this study. Should F-15 unit costs grow sufficiently to meet the projection based on the historical trend, confidence in the continuing applicability of this trend would be reinforced. The debate certain to follow could well be the last of its kind. With the cost trend reaffirmed, the prospect that the next generation of multipurpose fighters—that is, the replacement(s) for the F-15 and the F-14 that can be anticipated in the mid-1980s—will cost $100 million or more apiece (plus the cost of research and development and accessories, and an inflationary markup) would become entirely plausible. Merely to equip a single Air Force tactical squadron with this hypothetical "F-1985" would cost $3 billion (in current dollars). And a program on the same scale as the F-15 could cost $100 billion.

Perhaps the culprit is lack of imagination, but it is difficult to envision what arguments could be used to persuade the nation that expenditures on such a scale were justified. If this appraisal is correct, there will be essentially three courses open: reducing force levels, perhaps to a dozen wings or less spread among all the services; slowing the pace of modernization by postponing the introduction of the next design generation; and breaking away from the design philosophy that has been responsible for the cost bind by turning to specialized types of aircraft, pursuing a much more conservative approach to technological innovation, or both.

Indeed, as noted, the F-15 shows signs that the process of tempering traditional attitudes toward technological innovation may already have begun. The uncertain procurement future of the lightweight fighter, however, suggests that the Air Force is not yet ready to turn to specialized designs for every mission. But the disparity between the cost of the LWF and that of multipurpose fighters is so great that the pressures to consider greater use of specialized designs can only increase.

The Trend in Attack Aircraft

About one-third of the aircraft in the current U.S. combat inventory were designed primarily for attacking surface targets. In the Air Force the duties of these more specialized types (all are subsonic and considered to be limited in air combat capability) were assimilated following World War II by long-range fighters and the attack designation was discontinued. Since that time all the new designs of this kind have been developed by the Navy, although the Air Force has also adopted some for its use. Currently the Air Force has an operational strength of only 216 attack aircraft (Navy-designed A-7s), whereas the Navy and the Marine Corps together have over 700.

With the Air Force's attention directed toward developing multipurpose aircraft, the number of new attack designs has been comparatively low during the past twenty-five years, and most of these have been "light" attack types. The following analysis, which is parallel to that for fighters, is confined to the light attack variety.

The striking point that emerges from examining the cost trend in specialized attack aircraft, shown in Table 4-4 and Figure 4-3, is that the rate of increase for these types has been less than one-tenth the rate for multipurpose fighters.

Design Philosophy

This marked contrast again raises the basic question: how much mission versatility should be built into a single aircraft?

Proponents of versatility base their economic arguments on the advantages of minimum variety in the aircraft inventory, reasoning that designing one aircraft capable of carrying out a variety of different missions with

Table 4-4. The Evolution of U.S. Light Attack Aircraft

		Average flyaway cost[a] *(thousands)*				*Weight (thousands of pounds)*	
Aircraft	*Year first operational*	*Current dollars*	*Deflator*[b]	*Fiscal 1975 dollars*	*Number built*	*Empty*	*Gross*
A-20	1941	115	29.6	390	7,358	14	20
A-1	1948	254	39.7	640	3,160	12	24
A-4[c]	1956	522	52.6	990	2,500	9	24
A-7[c]	1967	2,200	68.8	3,200	1,536	15	37
A-10(A-X)[d]	1976[e]	2,450	109.9	2,200	729	19	46

Sources: Same as Table 4-1.
 a. Procurement cost of complete aircraft including airframe, engines, and avionics. Does not include cost of research and development, spare parts, or associated support equipment and facilities.
 b. Fiscal year 1975 = 100.
 c. In production. "Number built" is the number of aircraft in the announced procurement program as of March 1974.
 d. Estimated.
 e. Target date.

only minor modifications can lead to large savings in development costs, in production costs through economies of scale, and in operating and maintenance costs through standardization. The best publicized product of this approach has been the much criticized F-111 (TFX), though the most successful example is the F-4 Phantom II, which has served the Air Force, Navy, and Marine Corps in a variety of roles since the early 1960s.

The disadvantages of versatility in aircraft design are the same as those inherent in any sort of general purpose machine. First, while it can perform several different operations, it is generally less proficient at doing any single one than a machine designed specifically for that operation and no other would be. Second, a machine intended to perform several operations must have the performance qualities needed to satisfy the most demanding one, and when it is used where lesser performance would suffice, efficiency suffers from overdesign. As was discovered in Southeast Asia, the expensive qualities built into tactical aircraft to carry out deep penetration missions are not only unnecessary but can actually be a hindrance in performing close air support.[18]

The alternative to versatility and the multipurpose design philosophy is to design and build a wider variety of aircraft, each specialized to perform a single mission. Proponents of specialization argue that in most instances it would improve efficiency at both ends. Omitting many of the

18. Compared with modern high-performance jets, piston-engined A-1 Skyraiders performed so well in the close air support role over South Vietnam that the United States for a time considered reopening production of this then twenty-five-year-old design.

Figure 4-3. Trend in Unit Cost of U.S. Light Attack Designs

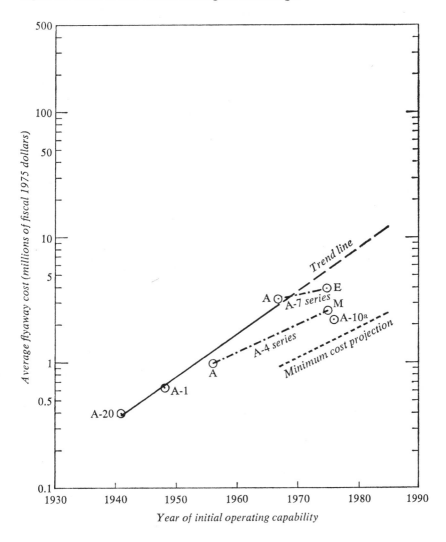

Sources: Same as Table 4-1.
a. Estimated.

expensive features built into the multipurpose type but not needed for any but the most demanding missions would lower costs, and since the special purpose aircraft would be designed for only one task, the performance characteristics most essential to carrying out that task effectively need not be compromised in the aircraft's design.

Critics of specialization point to two disadvantages. First, the economies that can be realized from standardization would suffer from greater variety in the aircraft inventory, although this tendency would be offset to the extent that the specialized aircraft displaced a portion of the more complex multipurpose types. Second, and potentially far more important, a certain loss in flexibility would be bound to result. Whereas multipurpose aircraft have some capability to perform each combat task on the tactical mission roster, specialized aircraft that excel in one mission are likely to have little capability for others.

The question of design is therefore closely linked to that of mission priorities. It is important that this be recognized and that a decision to convert any significant portion of the present force of multimission aircraft to specialized types be based on a reasonable confidence as to which missions will be most productive in the contingencies for which the United States wants to be prepared. It would be a serious error to entertain the simplistic notion that more is always better than fewer and that if three airplanes of one design can be bought and operated for the same cost as a single airplane of another design, that is what ought to be done. Nevertheless, the potential savings to be realized from specialization merit attention —despite the conflict of this approach with traditional USAF doctrine and despite the risks it might entail.

The two highly specialized combat aircraft now under development for the Air Force face an uncertain future. Each is less expensive to produce and operate than the aircraft preferred by the Air Force, and each represents a pronounced departure from traditional American warplane design. This becomes apparent when the costs of the lightweight fighter, specialized for battlefield air superiority, and the A-10, specialized for close air support, are compared with the historical cost trends.[19] The flyaway cost of producing a lightweight fighter with performance in aerial combat equal or superior to that of the F-15 is estimated at $2.5 million to $3.0 million if 700 are procured, only about 30 percent as much as the F-15 is estimated to cost under the most favorable assumptions. Similarly, the flyaway cost of the A-10 is officially estimated at about $2.2 million (exclusive of the new 30-mm cannon being developed in conjunction with the A-10 program), well below the cost of any warplanes in the current active Air Force arsenal.

The Air Force has no types designed exclusively for these battlefield

---

19. The divergence from traditional patterns is most obvious for the lightweight fighter but less so for the A-10, which is comparable to its specialized predecessors.

missions in its present inventory, relying instead on the residual capabilities inherent in aircraft designed for more demanding missions. The record to date suggests that the service might well prefer to continue this arrangement, viewing specialized designs as threats to its long-range multipurpose types.[20] The Air Force's limited enthusiasm for specialization now, it might be added, is in marked contrast to the services' position on the F-111, where both the Air Force and the Navy sought to specialize the design as much as possible for their respective, incompatible missions: deep penetration attack and carrier air defense.

An Ultimate Solution?

There is another possibility for breaking free of the historical cost trend, really a matter of carrying specialization one step further, which ought not to be overlooked although it appears unlikely that relief from this direction could be forthcoming in time to head off the crisis in unit costs that may otherwise arise in the 1980s. In addition to being multipurpose and incorporating all, or nearly all, the features prevailing technology had to offer, the aircraft designs described show a third familial trait: all carry a human crew. This is becoming an increasing encumbrance; it not only limits some facets of performance for advanced systems, but also accounts for a large share of the systems' cost. Getting the people out of the fighting vehicle is technology's greatest challenge and offers perhaps the best way of all to break out of the cost spiral in which manned U.S. designs seem to be trapped.

Unit cost could be expected to be much lower for unmanned aircraft (called remotely piloted vehicles, or RPVs) for several reasons: all the special features built into a manned aircraft solely to support and protect the lives of the crew could be eliminated, the aircraft could be built to relaxed tolerances and generally lower manufacturing standards, and on-board avionics could be simplified (most of the electronics gear would be carried aboard a "mother ship"). Smaller size, greater acceleration and maneuverability, and eventually, in perfected RPVs, perhaps greater responsiveness would all contribute to survivability. In some missions, such

20. The extent to which Air Force attitudes may be changing on this point is unclear. On the one hand, the concept of a lightweight fighter seemingly remains anathema to the majority of Air Force planners; on the other, service support for the A-10 appears to be rallying in the face of congressional opposition.

as attacking heavily defended ground targets, the expendability of unmanned vehicles might lead to improved capability as well.

Unmanned drones programmed to fly specific flight paths or controlled from outside the battle area have performed reconnaissance tasks successfully for some time, and research continues to find ways of adapting the same technique to more difficult attack and air combat missions. One of the effects technology has had on war is to push the combatants farther and farther apart. Remotely piloted vehicles are a logical extension of this and will undoubtedly play an increasingly prominent role. A great deal of effort will be required to perfect such systems, however, and progress is more apt to come gradually than to bloom dramatically upon some major discovery. Nonetheless, the lure of improved performance and lower costs (in both dollars and lives) makes this a worthwhile field in which to invest research resources.

CHAPTER FIVE

MISSIONS AND AIRPLANES

On the assumption that the factor most responsible for the rapid growth in the cost of warplanes is the close relation between design philosophy and mission priorities, it seems useful to examine the ways in which U.S. air power doctrine, with its emphasis on missions that require deep penetration into hostile airspace and on sea-based operations, places extraordinary demands on aircraft performance, demands that in turn encourage the costly design philosophy described.

The Mission Roster

What is meant by tactical air power? What military objectives does contemporary U.S. doctrine call upon it to accomplish and what sorts of aircraft are needed for these purposes?

Air power theorists have traditionally distinguished two general spheres of air operations: strategic and tactical. In the prenuclear era the objective of strategic air attack was to wear down the enemy's will and ability to resist by striking at the foundation of the socioeconomic structure—the morale of the civilian population and the means of production. Repeated attack by massive air armadas was the instrument used to advance these goals. Today, with the tremendous destructive potential of nuclear warheads and the high confidence each side enjoys in the ability of its delivery systems to penetrate the other's defenses, this objective is no longer relevant for the forces designated as strategic, however. Their mission has become deterrence. To the extent that the United States may still wish to pursue the old strategic objectives in a conventional conflict (and it is worth noting that the option is open only against a nonnuclear opponent), the task now falls on the tactical air forces.[1]

1. The high cost of strategic bombers would in most instances prohibit their sustained use to deliver conventional munitions against a formidable set of modern air

Unlike the strategic forces, U.S. tactical forces are charged with carrying out a variety of activities aimed for the most part directly at defeating the enemy on the battlefield. There are two noteworthy exceptions to the rule, however. The first is attacking enemy airbases and supporting ground facilities to gain air supremacy, and the second is endeavoring to interdict the flow of war matériel near its source. Both missions require penetration far beyond the immediate battle area and are now performed by highly sophisticated long-range fighter-bombers carrying larger bombloads than the four-engined B-17 Flying Fortresses of World War II. At this end of the mission roster, tactical operations have blurred into the sphere of activity once the exclusive reserve of the strategic forces.

Because the logic of procurement decisions on specific weapon systems is based on the priority given various missions, it seems worthwhile to describe the principal tactical mission areas.

The multiplicity of activities that current U.S. doctrine calls on the tactical air forces to perform may be grouped into five major mission categories: counterair, interdiction, close air support, airlift, and reconnaissance and electronic warfare. In addition, there are myriad support functions such as command and control, rescue, medical evacuation, and psychological warfare. Finally, there are the special operations that grew out of the unique character of the war in Southeast Asia—activities that may or may not find a permanent place in the Air Force mission structure.

COUNTERAIR. The mission of first priority for U.S. tactical air forces is to win and maintain air superiority, by which is meant the freedom to carry out other missions at an acceptable level of losses (and by the same token, deny the enemy this freedom). Of course what is "acceptable" is apt to vary a great deal with circumstance. This consideration, along with the important question of the extent of the geographic area over which freedom of operation is desired, give the term many gradations.

At one extreme, air supremacy means the ability to carry out a wide range of activities over hostile as well as friendly and contested areas with no more than nuisance interference from opposing air forces that have been destroyed, driven off, or otherwise incapacitated. This is the status U.S. forces enjoyed throughout the conflict in Southeast Asia, in Korea

---

defenses; the rate of bomber losses would outweigh the limited destructive effects of such payloads. Although B-52s were used extensively in a tactical role in South Vietnam and briefly in a strategic role over North Vietnam, tactical operations in South Vietnam were carried out with impunity (the communists had no antiaircraft weapons that could threaten the bombers), and the strategic operations over North Vietnam faced weak fighter defenses, lasted only twelve days, and were in any case motivated by urgent and unusual political circumstances.

earlier (though in a less than pure form because of the Manchurian sanctuary), and over most of Europe and the Pacific during the last year of World War II.

More modestly, the goal could be less than absolute supremacy over less than the entire theater—over only friendly or contested, not hostile, territory. In a conventional tactical environment, where a large number of air attacks are needed to have a decisive effect on the ground battle, this more limited degree of air superiority is much the same as maintaining a successful air defense. From the standpoint of aircraft performance requirements, the extent and degree of air superiority to which doctrine aspires is of critical significance.

INTERDICTION. Often misunderstood as an attempt to literally "strangle"[2] an enemy's forward ground forces by denying them even a subsistence level of logistical support, air interdiction is in fact less ambitiously aimed at constraining the military initiatives open to the enemy by reducing supplies for battlefield consumption, disrupting communications, inhibiting troop concentrations, and forcing the diversion of resources to protect rear areas. Interdiction efforts are sometimes further categorized as battlefield, forward, or deep depending on which segment of the enemy's lines of communication are attacked. Because the high costs of waging an interdiction campaign are evident and the benefits, if any, frequently are not, interdiction has for many years been the most controversial of the tactical missions.

CLOSE AIR SUPPORT. Tactical air forces make their most immediate contribution to the surface battle by enhancing the firepower of friendly ground forces through close air support. Munitions are delivered by air directly against the enemy's deployed combat forces, usually when they are in contact with, and hence in proximity to, friendly units. Critics of close air support view it as no more than an expensive augmentation to ordinary artillery fire support. Proponents point to responsiveness, accuracy, and more effective munitions as advantages worth the extra cost.

RECONNAISSANCE AND ELECTRONIC WARFARE. Aerial reconnaissance employs specially equipped aircraft to gather visual, photographic, and electronic intelligence data useful in selecting targets, appraising strike results, and positioning friendly forces. Missions purely for reconnaissance are flown in unarmed aircraft, usually modified fighter-bombers equipped with sensory gear in place of the usual weapons.[3] Electronic

2. Major interdiction campaigns in World War II and in the Korean War were assigned this code name.
3. Armed reconnaissance, in contrast, is carried out by loaded combat aircraft

warfare missions, also flown in unarmed aircraft, use electronic counter-measures to reduce the effectiveness of enemy air defenses, thereby facilitating penetration by the strike forces.

TACTICAL AIRLIFT. This is the movement by air of men, equipment, or supplies within the theater of operations, usually over distances of no more than a few hundred miles, often much less. Airlift increases the responsiveness of ground forces, both offensively and defensively, and in some instances may provide the only means of supporting exposed forward positions. Helicopters, as well as fixed-wing aircraft able to operate from marginal landing fields, are used for this.

As might be expected, there is a great deal of contention over the relative emphasis different missions should receive, and indeed whether some should not be discarded altogether. This issue cannot be resolved here. It is possible, however, to try to demonstrate the links between missions, costs, capabilities, and the types of aircraft in the tactical inventory.

The diversity of the missions charged to the tactical air forces is apparent. What is less frequently recognized is that each of these missions places different demands on aircraft performance. Besides knowing what task a particular aircraft is to perform (for tactical aircraft there are four possibilities: fighting other aircraft, attacking surface targets, gathering intelligence, or moving troops and supplies), it is critical for the designer to know where and under what conditions that task is to be carried out. Over the battlefield? And if so, in a "permissive" or a contested environment? Or deep over hostile territory, which implies a more threatening air environment and calls for longer range? Finally, how much capability to operate in bad weather should be built into a particular design? The answers to these questions determine not only what an aircraft will look like, but also how much it will cost and, through the mechanism of total-cost constraint, how many aircraft the tactical forces will have.

It becomes evident that the United States answers in a way different from other nations when its aircraft now in service are compared with those of its most powerful potential adversary, the USSR.

U.S. and Soviet Airplanes

Since the airplane came of age as an instrument of war in the 1930s, successive generations of American tactical warplanes have each been

---

that overfly hostile territory seeking targets of opportunity to attack. Because of the difficulty of locating targets on the ground from high-performance aircraft and their limited search time, armed reconnaissance by U.S. forces has declined.

larger, more complicated, and more costly than the aircraft of opposing nations. This historical generality is still true. Table 5-1 compares some of the vital statistics for the most popular U.S. designs now in use with those of the Soviet Union. In addition to physical characteristics (how much the design weighs, how much it can lift, and how far it can fly[4]), the year in which the basic design was first flown (or was first noted, in the case of the Soviet entries) and when it became operational are also shown, as is the approximate cost of producing the latest models. For the Soviet aircraft, the latter estimate is expressed in terms of what it is believed each design would cost to produce in the United States by U.S. methods and does not reflect its real cost or burden to the USSR, where technical manufacturing resources are less plentiful. In this context, it is useful to note that, although the Soviet Union has experimented with many more new aircraft designs since 1960 than has the United States, its tactical air forces continue to rely extensively on product-improved versions of aircraft developed in the mid-1950s. Because the United States introduces more of the new designs it develops, only 7 percent of U.S. tactical combat forces are still equipped with aircraft designs that were operational in 1960.

In contrast to the lightweight, short-range MIG-21, on which the Soviet Union has relied for counterair missions for the past ten years or so and on which, barring a crash effort to produce some new type, it is likely to remain reliant through most of the 1970s, the United States elects to build its counterair capability around a totally different kind of airplane. The mainstay of U.S. air superiority, the F-4 Phantom II, is nearly three times as heavy as and has nearly three times the range of its Soviet counterpart, and costs more than three times as much to produce.

The F-4 and the MIG-21 have met on numerous occasions over North Vietnam and in the Middle East. While the F-4 is generally considered to be the better system in aerial combat under most conditions, unlike the F-86 in Korea its record of performance against MIGs does not clearly establish justification for its greater cost. Although the unclassified information available does not permit an exact determination of the combat exchange ratio between the F-4 and the MIG-21, over North Vietnam it

---

4. The data shown in the table are "ferry" ranges. This is the maximum distance the aircraft can fly at optimum altitude and speed with the greatest amount of fuel aboard (internally and externally) it can carry but no munitions payload. The limit to the distance the aircraft can feasibly operate in a fighting capacity from its home base and return (its combat radius) depends on a number of very detailed technical specifics that vary with circumstance. In most cases, however, this distance would be little more than one-third the aircraft's ferry range.

Table 5-1. First-line Tactical Combat Aircraft of the United States and the USSR

Characteristic	Primary role, counterair		Primary role, surface attack				
	MIG-21 (USSR)	F-4ᵃ (U.S.)	SU-7 (USSR)	YAK-28ᵇ (USSR)	A-7 (U.S.)	A-6 (U.S.)	F-111 (U.S.)
Empty weight (thousands of pounds)	11	28	19	21	19	26	47
Lift capacity (thousands of pounds)	7	28	10	10	22	34	43
Maximum range (hundreds of nautical miles)	7	20	8	12	29	29	33
Design series first flown or seen	1956	1958	1956	1955	1965ᶜ	1960	1964
Initial operating capability	1960	1961	1960	1961	1967	1963	1967
Flyaway cost (millions of 1975 dollars)ᵈ	1.3	4.3	2.1	2.5	3.3	8.3	14.0

Source: *Jane's All the World's Aircraft: 1971–1972* (McGraw-Hill, 1971); *Aviation Week and Space Technology* (March 11, 1974), pp. 123, 134.
a. Also has a significant capability for attacking surface targets.
b. May also be configured as an all-weather interceptor.
c. The F8U fighter from which the A-7 design was derived first flew in 1955.
d. Unit cost of airframe, engines, and avionics. Does not include cost of research and development, spare parts, or associated support equipment. Costs of U.S. designs are derived from fiscal 1974 procurement of the F4E, A-70, A-6E, and F-111F. Costs of Soviet designs are author's estimates.

was probably between two and three to one in favor of the F-4.[5] By past standards, this was a disappointment, at best, and a source of some concern to many defense specialists.

5. During one short period for which data are available, the summer of 1972, F-4s downed 16 MIGs (including 4 older MIG-17s and -19s) at a cost of 11 F-4s: an average of 1.5 MIG kills for each F-4 lost. Through November 1972 the United States destroyed 170 North Vietnamese aircraft in aerial combat, sustaining a loss of 69 aircraft, for an overall exchange ratio of 2.5 to 1. Less than one-half of North Vietnam's losses consisted of MIG-21s, however, the rest being mostly obsolescent types (MIG-17s) of Korean War vintage. Not all the U.S. losses were F-4s, nor were all destroyed by MIG-21s. One explanation frequently put forth for this relatively poor showing is the disadvantageous environment in which U.S. penetrators had to fight. Although "MIG Alley" in Korea was also a highly unfavorable tactical situation for U.S. forces, this did not prevent their achieving a very favorable exchange ratio, including many kills against experienced Soviet pilots.

These differences in size, range, complexity, and cost between Soviet and U.S. designs are nearly as apparent in the several types whose principal mission is attacking ground targets. With the exception of the A-7, an exception not unnoted among American operating forces who have dubbed the aircraft "SLUF" (short little ugly fellow), the U.S. types are bigger, have greater range, and are more costly than their Soviet counterparts.[6]

Why is this so? It would be a mistake to condemn out-of-hand the penchant for buying big, costly aircraft as merely one more manifestation of American infatuation with size and gadgetry. Though none can say that this has not played some part, the American tradition can be explained in more tangible terms. At the heart of the matter is the something extra that the United States calls upon its tactical air forces to do. Whereas the Soviet Union and other nations that design and build tactical warplanes concentrate on developing capabilities applicable to the immediate area of the ground battle, the United States stresses the importance of being able to strike deep into hostile territory as well.

Deep Penetration Missions

A few historical statistics will demonstrate the long-standing order of priority in which the Air Force places different combat missions. As shown in Table 5-2, after achieving aerial dominance, as in Europe after Normandy and in Korea from the start, the Air Force devoted about half its combat effort to interdiction, a fourth to close air support, and the remaining fourth to continuing counterair operations.[7] With the air battle not yet won, as in the campaign to recapture Leyte in 1944, winning air superiority becomes the mission of overwhelming priority, and the close air support missions drop to near zero. By way of contrast, during the India-Burma campaign of 1944 and 1945 (under British overall command)

6. A similar comparison of U.S. types with those of Communist China would reflect even greater disparity. The Chinese Air Force is made up almost entirely of MIGs, the latest models, MIG-21s and MIG-19s (for ground attack), being Chinese-produced copies of Soviet designs bearing the same designations. These copies are generally considered inferior in reliability and performance to the Soviet originals. Moreover, a large portion of the Chinese fighter inventory, perhaps as much as two-thirds, is still composed of MIG-15s and -17s of Korean War vintage, many provided by the Soviet Union in the late 1950s, others copies made in China.

7. In Europe during World War II the close air support effort averaged only eleven sorties a day for each division engaged in the field.

Table 5-2. Mission Distribution of Air Force Tactical Effort
Sorties in thousands

Theater of operations	Counterair		Interdiction		Close air support		Total sorties
	Sorties	Percent	Sorties	Percent	Sorties	Percent	
Europe (June 1944– May 1945)	122.4	25	249.2	51	117.5	24	489.1
Pacific, Leyte campaign (October– December 1944)	11.1	80	2.6	19	0.2	1	13.9
Korea (June 1950– July 1953)	86.8	22	220.2	55	92.6	23	399.6

Source: U.S. Air Force Historical Division, *USAF Tactical Operations: World War II and Korea* (May 1962), pp. 51, 55, 120, 162.

over 60 percent of the 207,000 sorties flown by the Eastern Air Command (54 percent Royal Air Force, 46 percent Army Air Force) were for close air support and only 10 percent for interdiction despite the particular vulnerability of Japanese supply lines in this theater to air attack. No data have been made public that permit a mission breakdown of U.S. sorties in Southeast Asia, but it is likely that interdiction consumed an even larger fraction of the effort there than in World War II or Korea.[8]

The missions to which USAF doctrine has always assigned top priority are those that penetrate far into hostile airspace. Only the Marine Corps with its closely integrated division-wing teams gives first emphasis to supporting ground troops on the battlefield. The Air Force view seems to be that its tactical forces should concentrate on performing the tasks of which only the airplane is capable. Fire support may often be provided as well by artillery as by airplanes and at substantially lower cost, but only airplanes can reach targets far beyond the immediate battle area.

Deep penetration demands special qualities in the aircraft used. Not only must the attack aircraft be able to fly a long distance carrying a muni-

8. Interdiction almost certainly consumed at least three-fourths of the total U.S. fighter-bomber effort in Southeast Asia and possibly as much as 90 percent. The number of sorties flown in close support was limited by opportunity, however, and sparse communist opposition in the air reduced the requirement for counterair operations. Because there was little need to pick and choose among the alternative missions to which to apply the abundance of available air power, the statistics from Southeast Asia have less doctrinal significance than those from the earlier conflicts.

tions payload sufficient to make the trip worthwhile, it must also be prepared to cope with a variety of increasingly sophisticated area defenses en route and to deliver its payload accurately against point targets around which enemy air defenses are apt to be particularly intense and well organized (more so than in a fluid battle environment). Moreover, barring the use of nuclear weapons (which, it is important to note, the same kind of aircraft is equally capable of delivering), this feat must be accomplished again and again at a low long-run rate of attrition in the attacking force.[9]

Range and payload requirements alone are enough to ensure that deep penetration attack aircraft will be bigger, heavier, higher-powered, and more expensive than battlefield-oriented types. The requirement for complex avionics—navigation gear to find the target (with increasing emphasis on the ability to do so at night or in bad weather when enemy defenses are less effective), electronic equipment to counter radar and missiles, and complex fire control systems that permit bomb runs at high speeds and altitudes, thereby improving the chances of survival—boosts size, weight, and costs further, as do measures to protect the aircrew, which is likely to be captured if downed. All these features are less essential in aircraft not operating deep over hostile territory.

Emphasis on deep penetration affects the design of U.S. air superiority fighters in much the same way as it does the design of attack bombers and for much the same reasons. Historically, it has not proved an insurmountable task to hold air losses to acceptable levels against ground defenses alone even where, as over North Vietnam, these defenses include a profligacy of surface-to-air missiles and conventional antiaircraft weapons backed up by an elaborate radar control and warning network. For the foreseeable future, as in the past, the threat of intolerable losses is likely to become serious only where there are appreciable numbers of enemy interceptors in the target area.[10] Thus before long-range strike missions to

9. As observed earlier, there can be no set definition of what constitutes acceptable losses for offensive air operations. Very high loss rates have on occasion been tolerated for brief periods in order to strike targets deemed essential to the enemy. In most cases, however, a rate of attrition much higher than 2 percent (i.e., twenty aircraft lost for each thousand sorties flown) would quickly prove prohibitive, forcing curtailment or outright suspension of the offensive. Since it is not only the loss of aircraft that is important, but the loss of trained aircrews as well, the defense has a significant advantage because it can recover and return to service a much larger number of its downed aviators.

10. Initial reports of very high Israeli losses of U.S.-built aircraft to Soviet-built Arab missiles (mainly SA-6s and -7s) and light antiaircraft guns during the October 1973 war generated widespread alarm in the American press. Analysis of battle

interdict enemy lines of communication can proceed, it is considered necessary to destroy the other side's fighter defenses. To do this, enemy air forces must be met and defeated on or over their own bases, where all the tactical advantages are with the defense.

Carrying the air superiority battle deep into hostile territory means that U.S. fighters must not only be able to match the combat performance of the interceptors that rise to oppose them, but also have the same ability to survive long flights across heavily defended air space as that demanded of the strike aircraft. Since the qualities most useful in aerial combat—maneuverability, quick acceleration, and accurate weapons—are not altogether compatible with those necessary for deep penetration, the fighter designed for deep penetration must incorporate more than the usual number of compromises and becomes, virtually by definition, a multipurpose aircraft.

Whether the United States ought to continue paying a premium to preserve the deep penetration capability that the Air Force stresses so heavily, even if this means accepting a certain numerical inferiority to the Soviet Union, or would be better advised to redirect its resources all or in part

---

damage data suggests that the Israelis did comparatively better in the air than on the ground, however, retaining (aside from replacements) the same numerical balance in the air as at the onset of hostilities, while ground strength, measured in numbers of tanks and self-propelled (or assault) guns, deteriorated in relation to that of the Arab coalition.

Nor do Israeli air losses appear to have been excessive, considering the intensity of the action. On the conservative assumption that each of its combat aircraft flew an average of two sorties a day (a much lower rate than was achieved in the 1967 conflict), the overall combat loss rate was about 8 aircraft per 1,000 sorties, or a total of 105 aircraft lost in flying 13,000 sorties. For A-4s, the aircraft on which the Israelis rely most heavily for attacking ground targets and therefore the type one would expect to be exposed most frequently to the low-altitude missiles that many early accounts held to be so lethal, the loss rate appears to have been somewhat greater, between 10 and 15 aircraft lost for each 1,000 sorties flown.

While these rates are higher than the United States experienced in its bombing campaigns against North Vietnam (3.5 aircraft lost per 1,000 sorties in 1966, dropping to 3.1 in 1967 and only 1.5 in 1968 as more effective tactics and countermeasures were perfected), they are not extraordinary for a short surge effort. During the last seven months of World War II, for example, the allied First Tactical Air Force lost 316 aircraft in flying 48,800 sorties against weak air opposition over Europe—a loss rate of 6.5 aircraft per 1,000 sorties. If the Israelis, as is probable, achieved a higher utilization rate than assumed here, or if the sorties flown by the replacement aircraft sent to Israel are considered, the Israeli loss rate may well have been lower than this. Certainly, there is as yet no public evidence from the October 1973 war to suggest a decline in the survivability of tactical warplanes over the modern conventional battlefield.

toward accomplishing strictly battlefield functions depends on the answer to two sequential, and unfortunately quite technical, questions.

First, can a workable degree of air superiority, sufficient to protect friendly ground forces and to allow effective close air support, tactical airlift, and reconnaissance missions, be achieved over the battle area exclusively through aerial combat employing lightweight, short-range interceptors supported by mobile radar, communications, and antiaircraft equipment on the ground? Or is even this limited degree of operational freedom attainable only through major deep penetration attacks against enemy airbases?

If one accepts the feasibility of striving for limited battlefield air superiority without airbase attacks, then the case for continuing to configure tactical air forces with long-range aircraft hinges mainly on the worth of deep interdiction. This raises the second question: are air attacks on enemy communications likely in most contingencies to produce results commensurate with their costs? If not, a restructuring of U.S. land-based tactical air forces is logically in order.

Those who support the established position argue that, before tactical air power can significantly influence the ground battle, the battle for control of the air must be won. Warplanes, they note, are far more easily destroyed on the ground than in the air. They contend that opposing air forces can never be destroyed solely through aerial combat, however favorable the exchange ratio, because the enemy can always manage their losses by rising less often to fight. In contrast, by attacking airbases, as the Germans failed to do with determination in 1940 and 1941 during the Battle of Britain and as the Israelis did so successfully in 1967, total air supremacy comes within reach.

Critics doubt the relevance of the Israeli example for the United States, pointing out that against a reasonably alert defense exercising a modicum of caution airbases are among the most difficult of targets.[11] Damaged runways can be repaired in hours, and parked aircraft and key support facilities can be protected by dispersal and "hardening," either with low-cost surface shelters that must be destroyed one by one with direct hits (and individually may or may not actually contain an aircraft) or, if the terrain permits and the expense is warranted, by placement underground.

Those who would prefer to see U.S. tactical air power tailored more

---

11. The October 1973 conflict in the Middle East, when the Israelis were unable against prepared defenses to repeat their 1967 achievement in quickly destroying Arab air forces on their bases, tends to support this view.

closely to operations directly over the battlefield acknowledge that enemy air power cannot be totally eradicated without deep penetration airbase attacks but view such a goal as both too ambitious and unnecessary. In the contingency most influential in shaping U.S. planning for general purpose forces—that of an attack by the Warsaw Pact countries on NATO Europe —they believe that with the present air balance it would be unwise to strive for the sort of absolute air supremacy to which the United States has grown accustomed from past wars. (See Appendix B, the balance of air power in Europe.)

Moreover, they see the most likely prospect in a Warsaw Pact–NATO war as being an initial phase fought with conventional weapons lasting no more than a few weeks, ending, if not in a negotiated cease-fire, with an unavoidable escalation to nuclear warfare. Those who accept this "short war" assumption argue that the overriding military objective during this conventional phase of the conflict should be to minimize the ground given up to the communists, and the best way for air power to contribute to this objective is through close air support, the effect of which would be felt immediately in the ground battle. They therefore conclude that it would constitute a poor investment for the United States to divert resources from this mission in order to concentrate on winning air supremacy as a prelude to mounting an interdiction campaign that, however successful, could have only a marginal effect on the ground battle in so short a time.

Proponents of a battlefield-oriented tactical air force believe that close air support and battlefield reconnaissance and airlift missions could be carried out effectively behind a screen of lightweight fighters. They argue that very high aircraft losses must be anticipated in a major war in Europe whatever the counterair strategy, that a brief conflict will have to be fought with existing forces, and that the numerical inferiority that the United States accepts in opting for expensive deep penetration aircraft is a further disadvantage.

Also to be weighed is the possibility that restructuring U.S. tactical air forces might affect the strategic nuclear balance. Although the United States does not formally consider its tactical fighter-bombers part of its strategic nuclear arsenal, from the Soviet point of view this distinction must seem somewhat artificial. All U.S. land-based deep penetration aircraft (F-111s, F-4s, and the coming F-15) are capable of delivering multi-kiloton "tactical" nuclear warheads several hundred miles into European Russia from bases in Western Europe. The Air Force has over 1,300 such types in its operational squadrons, including nearly 500 forward deployed on British and European bases, and the Navy has another 400 (A-6s and F-4s), some of which, if carriers risked the hazardous waters of the North Sea or the eastern Mediterranean, could also reach Russian targets with a nuclear payload. Supporters of retaining the deep penetration character of the tactical air forces cite Soviet concern in the strategic arms limitation talks (SALT) over this strategic nuclear potential as evidence of their worth and believe that it would be unwise to weaken this deterrent by converting any part of the deep penetration forces to aircraft whose contribution would be limited to the conventional battlefield. Such a move, it is feared, might also work to encourage NATO allies to develop their own tactical nuclear capability.

Others see forward-based tactical fighter-bombers as contributing little to the strategic deterrent. They feel that U.S. strategic forces proper— U.S.-based B-52 and FB-111 bombers, Minuteman and Titan intercontinental ballistic missiles in hardened silos, and submarine-launched Polaris and Poseidon missiles—provide sufficient deterrent. They suggest that U.S. tactical air forces are a destabilizing factor because of their vulnerability to a variety of Soviet nuclear weapons when exposed on the forward bases from which they must strike. (The reasoning is that each side, aware of this vulnerability, has an incentive to strike first—the United States to realize the nuclear potential of the fighter-bombers before they are destroyed, and the Soviet Union to prevent this.)

Replacing deep penetration aircraft on forward bases with short-range battlefield types suitable only for delivering conventional munitions would eliminate this source of instability, thereby retarding somewhat the flashpoint of nuclear escalation, it is argued, at little sacrifice in U.S. capability to fight the tactical nuclear phase of a war in Europe should events develop this far. Although the United States would have substantially fewer nuclear-capable deep penetration tactical aircraft on D-day under this policy than it has now, holding those it did have in reserve in the United States would keep them safe during the opening conventional phase of a conflict, which would be fought instead by the forward-based close support and specialized counterair types. The smaller but intact force of deep penetration aircraft could be rapidly deployed to Europe if necessary. Such an action in itself could prove a useful signal to the Warsaw Pact countries.

The Aircraft Carrier

Any examination of the current tactical air structure would be incomplete without a discussion of a second way in which U.S. forces are unique: the extent of reliance on aircraft carriers. In terms of displacement, the U.S. fleet of attack carriers is four times as large as the fleets of the rest of the world combined; in terms of capability, the margin is still greater.[12] Currently the United States has three nuclear-powered carriers under construction, each of which will displace nearly 80,000 tons. The last carrier built outside the United States was completed in 1963—a conventionally powered 22,000-ton ship built in France.

The Soviet Union has never built a true aircraft carrier and has no experience whatever in the demanding field of carrier operations. Evidence suggests that it may be about to venture into sea-based tactical air operations, however, with two ships reportedly now under construction. Relatively small by U.S. standards (the Soviet carriers are variously reported as displacing 30,000 to 45,000 tons), it remains to be seen what use the USSR will make of these ships.[13] Their size and design suggest that they would be best suited for operating vertical or short-takeoff-and-landing (V/STOL) aircraft. If so, their role would probably be one of sea control (the use of short-range sea-based aircraft against surface warships) rather than of projecting air power ashore, which is the primary mission of the much larger U.S. carriers.

The key question is whether the Soviet Union intends to go beyond the kind of carriers now being built. On the one hand, these ships would be a logical intermediate step for acquiring technical data and experience if the ultimate goal is to build and operate large attack carriers. On the other hand, many analysts find it difficult to envisage a use for the attack carriers that would justify the tremendous costs of such a venture, not only of building ships and aircraft but also of acquiring the necessary technology and operational expertise.

12. The fourteen ships now in the U.S. fleet aggregate standard displacement of 780,000 tons. Other nations have seven carriers in commission that are capable of attack operations. Their aggregate displacement is 190,000 tons. See Raymond V. B. Blackman, ed., *Jane's Fighting Ships, 1972–73* (London: Jane's Yearbooks, 1972).

13. These ships might best be described as half carrier and half cruiser. The USSR also has a pair of new 15,000-ton helicopter cruisers, which might be used for antisubmarine or assault operations.

A second puzzling factor is that the Soviet Union is not known to have any aircraft suitable for carrier operations, either V/STOL or catapult-assisted. Research efforts have been noted on two designs, a short-takeoff variation of the SU-11 Flagon and a new YAK, "Freehand," with a vertical takeoff capability, but both are considered experimental, not production, prototypes. What is clear is that the USSR is a decade or more away from possessing either the fleet or the expertise to seriously rival existing U.S. capability for attack carrier operations in the seemingly unlikely event that it elects to pursue this goal.

The relative merits of land-based and sea-based air power, and how U.S. tactical air resources should be distributed between the two, have been long debated. At the heart of the controversy lies the uncontested observation that a carrier, including its aircraft, escorts, and auxiliaries, represents a great many national security eggs placed in one basket (over three billion dollars in initial investment and hundreds of millions each year in operating costs). Advocates on both sides of the debate agree that the mobility of carriers gives them a critical advantage over static land bases in some situations and that some carriers are needed. Argument arises over which situations, how many carriers, and what kind. These are complex issues;[14] only their most important aspects will be summarized here.

Part of the discussion centers on the survivability of the carrier. The second largest tactical air program for the 1970s, the F-14, has been justified by the Navy primarily on the ground that it will improve the chances of carrier survival against a sophisticated air attack. Defending a high-value point target such as an aircraft carrier against a coordinated attack by missile-launching bombers is an extremely difficult task. The critical element is time. Under the best of circumstances, the defense could expect no more than a few minutes in which to detect, identify, intercept, and destroy a subsonic bomber before its missile was launched.[15] Various tactics available to the offense would further reduce the probable reaction

---

14. They are treated at greater length in other Brookings studies: see Arnold M. Kuzmack, *Naval Force Levels and Modernization: An Analysis of Shipbuilding Requirements* (1971); and "Special Defense Issues: The Role of the Aircraft Carrier," in Charles L. Schultze, Edward R. Fried, Alice M. Rivlin, and Nancy H. Teeters, *Setting National Priorities: The 1972 Budget* (1971).

15. There is also the possibility of intercepting the missile itself, but this is more difficult still.

time allowed the carrier's defenses, and electronic countermeasures can be used effectively to gain precious additional seconds of survival for the attacker. In the worst case, there is the very real danger that the defense will simply become supersaturated—overwhelmed by many bombers jamming defensive radar and attacking along different azimuths. The carrier's best defense against this threat is its mobility, which makes it difficult for the enemy to establish the ship's position with sufficient accuracy to coordinate such an attack. However, improved surveillance techniques may be eroding this form of protection.

If design criteria are met, a number of the F-14's high-technology features will contribute significantly to easing the critical burden of time on carrier air defenses. The aircraft's swing wing will permit it to remain airborne longer, anticipating attack, making it less likely that time will be lost in "scrambling" and climbing to target altitude. But the key to the success of the system is the radar, computers, and Phoenix missiles that the F-14 will carry. These allow a single F-14 to engage up to six targets in rapid sequence and at very long ranges.[16] Unlike all existing intercept systems, the F-14 Phoenix need not close on its targets individually or at specific altitudes.

All these characteristics increase not only the probability that a given target will be intercepted but also the distance at which initial interception may be expected. On the assumption that the Phoenix, once fired, is no less effective than existing missiles, earlier interception will increase the probability of a target's being destroyed by allowing a better chance for reattack should the first attempt fail.

In view of the technical deficiencies experienced with many far less sophisticated weapon systems, which in some cases persisted well after a system was declared operationally ready, a certain skepticism remains about how the F-14/Phoenix will measure up to these ambitious performance goals in the field. If it does well, clearly it will be a valuable addition to carrier air defenses.

But this is not the only issue. A more fundamental one concerns the range of application and the utility of the carrier itself: specifically, what is the worth of the striking power the Navy's large attack carriers could deliver in the event of a conventional conflict with the Soviet Union?

The highly sophisticated, intense air attack that the F-14 is designed to

16. The builder of the Phoenix claims the system has successfully intercepted and theoretically destroyed a supersonic target drone at a range of over one hundred miles.

counter could be mounted at present only by the Soviet Union. Moreover, there is little chance that a threat will arise from another sector in this decade more severe than the Soviet threat of the past decade—against which, the Navy consistently maintained, the F-4 provided adequate protection. If the Navy was right about the survivability of carriers in the European theater during the 1960s, there should be no requirement for F-14s to protect carriers operating outside this theater during the 1970s.

In a nuclear encounter, the survival of carriers beyond the initial launching of their strike aircraft would not be essential. In such a conflagration, all military assets must be considered expendable or, at least, not reusable. By contrast, in a conventional conflict a carrier's contribution would depend on the total number of strike sorties it was able to launch, and this would vary with the carrier's life expectancy.

On the assumption of a maximum effort and at least thirty days of warning to mobilize and deploy, U.S. carrier-based aircraft could probably carry out 300 combat sorties daily in a major war in Europe,[17] well under one-tenth the number the United States and its NATO allies could stage from land bases. To reach front line targets in central Germany, where the heaviest (and probably decisive) fighting during the first few weeks would presumably take place, the aircraft carriers would have to operate in confined waters, either the North Sea or the Mediterranean, exposed to attack by submarines and missile-armed surface ships as well as by the long-range bombers that the F-14 has the primary mission of countering. Even then, the carrier aircraft would be operating at maximum range and consequently minimum effectiveness. Each carrier sunk or disabled would reduce the sea-based tactical air effort by 20 percent.

If one believes, given these constraints, that the carrier, if it can survive, still has a cost-effective contribution to make in a short conventional encounter with the Warsaw Pact countries, that the F-14 will substantially improve carrier air defenses, and that this will markedly improve the carrier's chances for survival, then the F-14 program is worthwhile; indeed, a somewhat larger purchase than the one announced may be justified. If one denies any of these premises, the F-14 is not needed and prompt termination of the program is in order.

17. This assumes a twelve-carrier fleet, of which nine would be available for sea duty, and that, of these, five would be configured for attack operations and committed to the European theater. Each of the five would have six squadrons of aircraft capable of averaging one sortie a day.

Marine Tactical Air Forces

Unlike the Army, which is largely dependent on a separate service for air support, the Marine Corps directly controls its own tactical air power.[18] This arrangement is justified by the principal mission of the Marines, which is to storm and seize hostile coastal areas by amphibious assault. As the Corps points out, this constitutes one of the most complex and, against resolute opposition, potentially hazardous maneuvers in modern war. Not only is the promise of prompt and absolute local air superiority over the landing area considered an indispensable precondition for such a venture; the degree of coordination between air and surface forces in breaching enemy defenses may well govern its outcome.

The Marine Corps contends that the required coordination can best be achieved through closely integrated air and surface forces. Hence, each of the three active, and the single reserve, Marine amphibious forces (MAFs) includes one air wing and one division as well as initial support elements. Each air wing is equipped with about 140 combat aircraft—twice the number contained in a USAF wing—and 180 support aircraft, mainly troop-carrying helicopters.

Although all elements of the Marine Corps are specifically trained, equipped, and organized to carry out amphibious assaults against contested shores, it is extremely unlikely that events would call for committing the entire force in this way. In fact, Marines have been used only once in an opposed over-the-beach assault since World War II—the Inchon landing of September 1950—and only six battalions (two-thirds of a division) went ashore then.[19] Even if some future contingency should require mounting a similar operation on a larger scale, shortages in appropriate sea lift would make it impossible to employ more than half the present active force in such a capacity. The bulk of whatever Marine forces might

18. The Corps remains reliant on the Navy, however, to provide the aircraft carrier bases and, if necessary, air reinforcements during the initial phase of an amphibious assault.

19. The interventions in Lebanon in 1958 and the Dominican Republic in 1965 were "administrative" landings, with most of the troops disembarking through prepared port facilities. Little special training or equipment and no air support are required for operations of this kind, which could be carried out by ordinary ground forces. The limited across-the-beach landings in South Vietnam in 1965 may have yielded some tactical advantages (though minor, as evidenced by the lack of contact), but they also had ceremonial overtones.

be committed to a future conflict would probably serve, as was the case in both Korea and Southeast Asia, in much the same way as the Army's infantry divisions.

It is not necessary, therefore, to challenge either the special requirement for air support during amphibious assaults or the current level of Marine surface forces to question whether the Marine Corps needs to maintain all the tactical air forces it now has. If one or more Marine divisions are likely to be deployed alongside Army divisions in Central Europe (as NATO planners assume) or to operate once again as elite infantry somewhere in Asia, a strong case can be made for a more efficient arrangement that would consolidate the air support responsibility for these divisions within the Air Force, with the Marine Corps retaining only enough air wings to support the surface forces that might actually be used in amphibious assault operations.

CHAPTER SIX

ALTERNATIVE TACTICAL
AIR PROGRAMS

This chapter will illustrate how different positions on the issues raised and discussed in the preceding analysis could affect the structure and costs of tactical air forces through the 1970s. To do this four alternative tactical air programs have been constructed.

As shown in chapter 3, at a projected cost of $141 billion (in fiscal 1975 dollars) through 1980, current programs will maintain approximately constant combat force levels while providing enough modernization to reequip one-third of today's fighter and attack squadrons with new aircraft. Investment in new weapons is dominated by spending for the F-15, which reaffirms the Air Force's doctrinal emphasis on deep penetration missions to achieve air supremacy and interdict enemy lines of communication, and the F-14, which indicates continuing confidence in the usefulness and survivability of aircraft carriers in any conventional confrontation involving the Soviet Union. Lesser programs under way will improve the capacity of existing forces to provide close air support (the A-10) and, toward the end of the decade, will begin to modernize the intermediate-range airlift forces (the advanced medium short-takeoff-and-landing transport—AMST).

As yet, there is no hint of any plan to reduce present tactical capabilities, which many argue is warranted in an era of relaxed international tension. But neither is there an indication of any intent to build up tactical air power as a substitute for ground forces, which others argue would be consistent with the Nixon Doctrine's call for greater reliance on American technology and less on American manpower.

No effort will be made to pass judgment on present policy or to advocate a specific alternative. Whether one considers the present course excessive, inadequate, lopsided, or just right will depend on how one appraises U.S. interests and perceives threats to them, the ways one believes tactical air power can promote these interests or counter these threats, and the kinds of forces one sees as best suited to doing so. More fundamental still is how much one is willing to spend to attain the confidence that the forces provided will be sufficient to accomplish what is expected.

Each of the four alternatives to the projected course of present policy is constructed around a central theme.

Option A calls for slower modernization with no change from the force levels projected for present policy or its mission priorities.

Option B suggests an extensive reordering of traditional mission priorities, deemphasizing those that require penetrating deep into hostile airspace in favor of a much improved capability to support ground troops on the battlefield, again with no change in the level of forces.

Option C would achieve a smaller force by eliminating the conventional deep penetration missions altogether, limiting the role of large attack carriers, and balancing Marine air strength with amphibious capabilities.

Option D would place increased reliance on tactical air power as a substitute for ground forces with faster modernization of the deep penetration and sea-based air forces and further expansion of close support forces.

The object here is to illustrate what sort of force structure would be consistent with each of these strategies, which of the new weapons now being considered would fit the strategy and which would not, and how costs and mission capabilities would vary with each. Although each alternative "packages" a considerable number of explicit decisions on weapons and forces, it is the thrust of these decisions rather than the details of their execution (necessary primarily for estimating costs) that is most significant.

Option A: Slower Modernization

The case for slowing the pace of modernization rests on the contention that because progress in weapons technology no longer provides real improvements in performance as quickly as in the past the introduction of new systems should be spaced out, awaiting some major technological breakthrough or at least an accumulation of lesser innovations sufficient to ensure that the new system will add enough capability to justify its greater cost. In other words, the historical American bias in giving the benefit of the doubt to innovation would give way to a more cautious approach, wherein the burden of proof would be placed on the new system, with large-scale procurement awaiting the outcome. It is worth noting that signs of movement in the direction of a slower but surer approach to weapons acquisition are already apparent in the guise of "competitive fly-offs," "fly before you buy" policies, and the "design to cost" dictate.

Lessening tension between the United States and the Soviet Union—the only adversary against which having an F-14 or F-15 in place of an F-4 might make a decisive difference for many years to come—could also be cited in support of a slower modernization policy. Postponing modernization incurs some additional risk of being caught in the early stages of a future conflict with aircraft not fully adequate to meet the task at hand. Proponents of slower modernization might acknowledge this risk but argue that it is acceptable since only the Soviet Union has the resources to pose such a danger and that a vigorous U.S. research and development effort, preserving the option of introducing new aircraft should Soviet forces suddenly appear to have large numbers of new weapons, could further mitigate that risk. Although the Russians develop and test many new designs, however, comparatively few progress beyond the experimental stage, and their operating forces are still equipped largely with aircraft of basic designs first introduced in the 1950s.

Against a slower modernization policy, it could be argued that, even with the advanced U.S. prototypes kept ready for production, with critical tooling at hand, and with Soviet forces closely monitored for the appearance of new weapons, two years or more might elapse before a new U.S. weapon could reach the operating forces in significant numbers; that even then combat efficiency would suffer for a time while aircrew and support personnel became proficient in working with the new design; and that this is an unacceptable delay. Underpinning this position is, of course, a presumption that the all-new weapons would prove markedly superior to the product-improved systems with which the operating forces would be equipped under Option A.

Another argument against slower modernization is that part of the savings, which accrue mainly in the investment account, are illusory over the long term since they reflect expenditures deferred rather than outright reductions. Sooner or later the F-4 will have to be replaced, if not in this decade, in the next, so that money saved in the 1970s will have to be spent in the 1980s. While this argument is valid to a point, it is nonetheless true that real and permanent savings accumulate with the lower average annual budgets that result from lengthening the period of the new weapons introduction cycle.

Further procurement of both the F-14 and the F-15 would be halted under this option. The 172 production models of the F-14A that have already been funded (through fiscal 1974) are sufficient to form and sustain six operational squadrons, one for each of the carriers that could be promptly committed to the European theater, where the threat to the ships is greatest. Alternatively, these squadrons could be doubled-up aboard the two or three carriers the Navy might be willing to risk in particularly dangerous waters such as the eastern Mediterranean (where evasion would be especially difficult and the ships would be exposed to the full array of Soviet anticarrier weapons). Procurement of Phoenix missiles would be cut back in proportion to the reduced number of F-14s.[1]

For air defense against the lesser threat faced by carriers operating in the Pacific, the Navy would rely on the same improved, more maneuverable version of the F-4 that the Marine Corps at one time selected in preference to the F-14 for its air wings. The Corps would receive no F-14s under this option but would also modernize with the improved F-4. These aircraft, equipped with the latest, longer-range Sparrow and Sidewinder missiles, would substitute for the Air Force's F-15 as well. In all cases, the rate of introduction of the improved F-4 would be gradual, geared to the operating attrition of the earlier models.

The present development programs for both the F-14 and the F-15, including the effort to perfect more powerful engines, would be brought to completion. Funds would be provided to carry out a protracted flight testing program for the F-15 aimed at further refining the design. Critical production tooling would be bought and maintained. The ninety-two F-15s already procured would be placed in two training squadrons to acquire operations data and form an expansion base should Soviet actions eventually dictate full-scale production.

Continued reliance on the improved F-4 in place of the F-14 and F-15, including cancellation of anticipated reconnaissance versions of both types, would produce a net saving in major weapons acquisition costs of $8.2 billion (in fiscal 1975 dollars) from 1975 to 1980.[2] Unless the F-14

1. The Navy argues that the required number of Phoenix missiles is independent of the number of F-14s procured (although no other aircraft can carry Phoenix) but is determined instead by the number of enemy aircraft in the threat to the carriers. This argument can be challenged on several grounds, not the least of which is its failure to consider diminution of the threat resulting from the destruction of enemy aircraft by the F-4s that would be retained if fewer F-14s were bought.

2. Estimated gross savings of $13 billion from halting further procurement of the F-14/Phoenix and F-15 systems, including the projected expansion initiatives asso-

and F-15 prove much more expensive to operate and maintain than is now expected, only minor savings in operating costs, probably little more than $200 million through 1980, would be generated by this move, however. There would be additional operating savings, estimated at $400 million, in the reserve forces, which would receive expensive-to-operate F-4s from the active duty forces at a slower rate under this option than under the present course.

Neither the lightweight fighter nor the A-10 has a direct counterpart in the present forces. Therefore the question whether to introduce these types is one of mission priorities (treated in the following option) rather than the pace of modernization. In this analysis of the most likely course of present policy, it has been assumed that the A-10 would be introduced into the existing force level largely as a replacement for the A-7 and that, consistent with past USAF preferences, the lightweight fighter would not be procured. These assumptions need not be altered by the slower approach to modernization postulated for this option.

Further economies would be realized by canceling the Air Force program to develop a pure-jet alternative to the C-130, the AMST, and the Marine Corps venture to develop an immediate successor (the AV-16) to its AV-8 Harrier. Termination of the AMST program would rest on the argument that the highly successful C-130 will remain fully adequate for the heavy tactical airlift role for the foreseeable future. This move could produce savings of $1.5 billion through 1980.

The $600 million (in fiscal 1975 dollars) program to equip four Marine light attack squadrons with the Harrier is barely completed, yet the Corps has already begun to press for a replacement before the end of the decade. In view of the earlier ardor with which the Corps endorsed the efficacy of the Harrier against the skepticism of many analysts as to the design's cost-effectiveness, calling so soon for a replacement seems difficult to justify. Cost projections for the present course include $700 million to fund the AV-16, if initial procurement begins in 1979. Under this option no AV-16s would be procured and the research and development program would be reduced to $200 million through 1980.

A final $300 million saving in major systems investment under this option would result from reducing the size of the airborne warning and control system (AWACS) aircraft procurement program from thirty-four

---

ciated with these programs ($6.0 billion saved on the F-15, $2.8 billion on the F-14A/ Phoenix, $2.4 billion on the F-14B, and $1.8 billion on the expected RF-14 and RF-15 spin-offs), less $4.4 billion in additional F-4 procurement and $400 million to maintain a standby production capacity for the F-15.

to twenty-four units. Originally intended primarily to serve the strategic defensive forces, the Air Force's arguments in support of the AWACS have gradually shifted to emphasis of its tactical role. Reducing the size of the AWACS program would acknowledge this change in mission and provide one AWACS aircraft for each Air Force tactical fighter wing. No AWACS aircraft would be procured for strategic defense against manned bombers.

The $1.0 billion program now under way to develop an improved, longer-range Sparrow missile for general use would continue unchanged: the need to correct deficiencies in existing air-to-air missiles is widely acknowledged. Also unchanged from the projections for the present course is procurement of the F-5E for U.S. allies and procurement of two additional aircraft carriers for the Navy by the end of the 1970s, a necessary first step if a twelve-ship force is to be sustained through the 1980s. These carriers would be the smaller, less costly types proposed by Secretary of Defense James R. Schlesinger in his annual report for fiscal year 1975 rather than the $1 billion Nimitz-class carriers that the Navy is now constructing.

U.S. capabilities under this option would differ very little from those expected under the present course in the next several years. The principal feature of this option, continued reliance on the F-4 for long-range counterair duties, carries some risk of a lessened capability for deep penetration strikes toward the end of the decade, since achieving the degree of air superiority prerequisite to such activity, already less than certain in any situation involving the Soviet Union, might become more difficult without a significant number of F-14s and F-15s. In return for acceptance of this risk, the severity of which is placed in better perspective by the observation that the current course will still leave 60 percent of the air combat forces equipped with unimproved F-4s, the slower modernization policy outlined in this option would trim the projected tactical air budget by $12 billion to $13 billion, or about 9 percent, over the next six years. The budget under this option, which would average about $2 billion a year less than the amount that has been requested for 1975, is summarized in Table 6-1.

Option B: Reordered Mission Priorities

The second alternative to the present course retains the proposals for slower modernization of the Navy and Marine Corps set out in Option A, and calls as well for a fundamental reorientation of the tactical combat

Table 6-1. Projected Costs of Tactical Air Forces under Option A, Slower Modernization, Fiscal Years 1975–80

Billions of fiscal 1975 dollars

Type of cost	1975	1976	1977	1978	1979	1980	1975–80 Total	Change*
Investment	8.7	7.4	7.0	7.3	7.6	7.6	45.6	−12.1
Major systems	3.8	2.9	2.6	3.0	3.3	3.3	18.9	−11.5
Other	4.9	4.5	4.4	4.3	4.3	4.3	26.7	−0.6
Operations	13.7	13.8	13.8	13.8	13.8	13.9	82.8	−0.6
Active forces	6.0	6.1	6.0	6.0	6.0	6.0	36.1	−0.2
Reserve forces	1.2	1.2	1.3	1.3	1.3	1.4	7.7	−0.4
Indirect support	6.5	6.5	6.5	6.5	6.5	6.5	39.0	0
Total	22.4	21.2	20.8	21.1	21.4	21.5	128.4	−12.7
Change*	−1.2	−1.9	−1.8	−1.9	−2.8	−3.1	−12.7	...

Source: Author's estimates.
a. From projected present program.

elements of the Air Force away from the deep penetration missions for which they are now configured (every tactical warplane in the current USAF inventory has a capability for attacking surface targets deep within hostile territory) toward missions supporting ground forces in the immediate battle area. This reorientation, which represents a greater departure from present policy than does slowing modernization, would be accomplished by replacing nearly all the existing force of multipurpose F-4s with less complex A-10s specialized for close air support and lightweight fighters specialized for counterair operations over the battlefield, rather than modernizing the F-4 force gradually with equally versatile F-15s, as projected under current policy, or improved F-4s, as proposed under Option A.

Such a course offers greater potential budget savings in the long run (including the years that lie beyond the forecast period) than can be achieved by merely slowing modernization, because the new specialized aircraft could be built and operated more cheaply than both new (the F-15) and existing (the F-4) multipurpose aircraft.

As noted earlier, the importance USAF doctrine assigns to interdicting rear area lines of communication has been the factor most instrumental in shaping the composition of the present force. For a deep interdiction campaign to proceed at an acceptable loss rate, it is necessary first to gain control of the air over hostile areas. This requires long-range fighters, such as the F-14 and F-15, capable of defeating the enemy's fighters over their own bases as well as of making concentrated attacks on these bases. All these operations must be carried out in an environment highly favorable to the other side, and they demand performance qualities that have made U.S. aircraft far more expensive on the average than those of other nations.

The Air Force could be expected to oppose the changes proposed under this option. Not only does the notion of air power limited principally to supporting ground forces smack of lowered status; also at stake is the cherished maxim that the first task of an air force is to vanquish opposing air forces. Without the means of striking an enemy's air force on its bases (neither the A-10 nor the lightweight fighter would have the deep penetration capability needed for this), the United States would have to settle for relative air superiority over local battle areas rather than the theater-wide domination.

Critics of the "win the air battle first" doctrine respond that it is unrealistic to expect to achieve prompt air supremacy in Europe and question the wisdom of designing the tactical air forces for this purpose at the expense of a lessened capability to provide battlefield fire support for ground forces. Such support or its absence could become the decisive factor in the critical opening phase of a conventional attack on Western Europe.[3]

Local battlefield air superiority, achieved through aerial combat employing lightweight fighters, would enable the United States to exploit the improved capability for close air support that the A-10 should provide and deny the enemy the same capability. With the enemy still in control of their own air space, deep penetration missions to interdict rear area lines of communication and weaken socioeconomic war-making potential without resorting to nuclear weapons would in all likelihood prove prohibitively costly in aircraft attrition.

In any event, shifting the composition of U.S. forces toward specialized designs means there would be not only fewer aircraft to strive for air supremacy, but also fewer aircraft suitable to exploit this supremacy, once achieved, through deep interdiction and attacks on enemy industry and morale. To rationalize the redirection in mission priorities that accom-

---

3. See Appendix B. The Warsaw Pact countries could commit 6,000 or more aircraft to the air battle against a NATO total of fewer than 4,000 (each side also has several hundred additional attack aircraft with very limited air combat capability). The Soviet-designed fighters lack the range to wrest control of the air from the allies over NATO-held areas but could operate defensively to challenge NATO air superiority over the battlefield and communist-occupied areas.

panies this option, therefore, it is necessary to accept the contention that the military advantages to be expected from deep interdiction missions are not worth the cost of continuing to maintain the capability to carry out these missions on a large scale with conventional munitions.

The utility of retaining some aircraft capable of deep penetration to deliver tactical nuclear weapons is a separate question, which opens a whole new field of debate. Here it is assumed desirable to preserve such a capability by retaining two wings of F-111s and an equal force of F-15s and F-4s for long-range escort duties. Augmenting the Air Force F-111s, F-15s, and F-4s for deep penetration strikes against select, high-value targets would be the A-6s and F-4s operating from the Navy's carriers.

As in the preceding option, procurement of the F-15 would be halted immediately, but unlike Option A, no effort would be made to maintain a standby production capacity for the F-15. Instead, the Air Force would expedite its development of the lightweight fighter, procuring 1,200 between fiscal 1976 and 1980 at a cost of $3.5 billion (in fiscal 1975 dollars). These aircraft would be formed into nine wings, replacing an equal number of F-4s. Procurement of the A-10 would be increased to support a seven-wing force by 1980. Rather than replacing only A-7s, as projected under the present course, the A-10s would also replace F-4s. The active A-7 force would be retained, though reduced to two wings by 1980.

By 1980 the Air Force would be virtually fully modernized (fifty of its projected sixty-six squadrons having been reequipped with aircraft of totally new design). Eighty percent of the force (nine wings of lightweight fighters, seven of A-10s, and two of A-7s[4]) would be oriented toward battlefield support missions; the remaining 20 percent would retain a deep penetration capability—a reversal of the mission emphasis projected for 1980 under the current course.

The proposal here to rapidly convert the Air Force F-4 wings to lightweight fighters and A-10s with no change in force levels would cost about $1.6 billion more in major weapons investment than the gradual modernization of the same wings with improved F-4s proposed in Option A ($4.1 billion as against $2.5 billion) but still be $1.9 billion less than the cost of partially modernizing these wings with F-15s, which is now planned. Deemphasis of deep penetration missions would permit modest reductions in the strength of the Air Force's reconnaissance and electronic

---

4. The optimum ratio of battlefield attack aircraft to screening lightweight fighters remains to be worked out. The analysis assumes a one-to-one ratio. Overall costs would be little affected by readjustments of the fighter-attack combination.

warfare units (an action inconsistent with the rationale for Option A), which would produce additional investment savings of about $0.9 billion (mainly from a cancellation of the EF-111 project). Moreover, by 1980 the Air Force's annual operating budget would be pared by an estimated $400 million. By contrast, slower modernization would produce only marginal savings in operating costs compared to the projections for current policy. The cost of operating the reserve forces, which would be receiving F-4s at a faster rate under this option, would be about $150 million a year higher by the end of the decade than estimated under the present course.

The budget for this option through fiscal 1980, on the assumption that the same actions are taken to slow the modernization of Navy and Marine combat squadrons and Air Force airlift squadrons as those postulated in Option A, would be as shown in Table 6-2.

Option C: Reduced Force Levels

Under Option B most of the budget savings that accompanied deemphasis of missions requiring a large number of aircraft with a deep penetration capability were reinvested to greatly improve the Air Force's close air support capability. Alternatively, these savings could be applied directly to reduce the defense budget. Downgrading the importance of conventional deep interdiction, and the attendant doctrine of air supremacy, would permit a one-third reduction in the number of tactical fighter wings at little sacrifice in the Air Force's capacity to provide air support to ground forces as it is projected to increase under current policy.

The smaller but fully modernized fourteen-wing force proposed under this option would be reached by complementing the five wings of A-10 close support aircraft the Air Force plans to procure with a five-wing force of lightweight fighters to provide air cover. Four wings of deep penetration aircraft would be retained for tactical nuclear missions, as in Option B, but would be fully modernized with two wings of F-111s and two of F-15s.[5] All of the Air Force's F-4s would be phased out by 1980, replacing F-100s in the Air National Guard. As under the current plan, all A-7s would also be placed in reserve status.

Prompt action to begin restructuring could generate substantial savings

5. This requires the procurement of 160 F-15s in fiscal 1975 and 1976 not included in Option A or B (at a cost of $1.9 billion).

Table 6-2. Projected Costs of Tactical Air Forces under Option B, Reordered
Mission Priorities, Fiscal Years 1975–80
Billions of fiscal 1975 dollars

| | | | | | | | 1975–80 | |
Type of cost	1975	1976	1977	1978	1979	1980	Total	Change^a
Investment	8.3	7.3	7.5	8.1	7.8	7.7	46.7	−11.0
Major systems	3.4	2.8	3.1	3.7	3.5	3.4	19.9	−10.5
Other	4.9	4.5	4.4	4.4	4.3	4.3	26.8	−0.5
Operations	13.7	13.9	13.9	13.8	13.7	13.5	82.5	−0.9
Active forces	6.0	6.1	6.1	5.9	5.8	5.6	35.5	−0.8
Reserve forces	1.2	1.3	1.3	1.4	1.5	1.6	8.3	+0.2
Indirect support	6.5	6.5	6.5	6.5	6.4	6.3	38.7	−0.3
Total	22.0	21.2	21.4	21.9	21.5	21.2	129.2	−11.9
Change^a	−1.6	−1.9	−1.2	−1.1	−2.7	−3.4	−11.9	...

Source: Author's estimates.
a. From projected present program.

in operating as well as investment costs through fiscal 1980. If the
fourteen-wing level were reached by the end of 1978 and the final conversion of the last remaining F-4 squadrons to lightweight fighters were
completed in 1980, operating savings of over $6 billion could be accu-
mulated. By the end of fiscal 1980, when the full savings from the proposed actions would be in effect, net recurring savings in operating costs
would amount to an estimated $1.7 billion (a saving of nearly $2 billion a
year in active duty operating costs less an increase of about $200 million
a year in higher costs for the F-4–equipped reserves). Investment spending for the Air Force would be $5 billion to $6 billion less through 1980
under this option than estimated under the present course.[6] By 1980 the
annual Air Force tactical investment budget would be nearly $2 billion
lower than the amount required to support the force structure projected
under the current course.

The size of the Navy's tactical air forces is determined by the number
of attack carriers in the fleet and the ratio of air wings to carrier "decks."
Under the present course the number of attack carriers will decline to
twelve from the level of fifteen projected for the end of fiscal 1975. The
Navy also has three smaller carriers used solely for antisubmarine (ASW)

6. This estimate includes economies associated with reducing the reconnaissance
and electronic warfare force in line with the reduction in deep penetration capability,
trimming the number of AWACS aircraft procured to seventeen, and retaining the
C-130 instead of beginning to modernize the airlift forces with the AMST. No
change in the airlift force level is postulated.

operations that will be retired shortly and not replaced; their operations will be transferred to the attack carriers. The Navy has always maintained one attack air wing for each attack carrier and one specialized ASW air wing for each ASW carrier.

In the preceding two options no change in either the number of carriers or the number of air wings from the levels projected under the present course has been assumed. However, a less expansive view of the role of the large attack carrier, limiting its operations to the Pacific and a minimum peacetime presence in the Mediterranean, would predicate a reduction to nine or fewer ships. The supporting argument for such a move is that the contribution to be expected from carrier-based aircraft in the NATO theater would not be sufficient, even under the most favorable assumptions, to justify the great cost of trying to protect these ships from the sophisticated, multifaceted threat the Soviet Union could pose.

Reducing the number of attack carriers to nine while continuing the scheduled modernization with nuclear-powered Nimitz-class ships and maintaining one full attack air wing for each would produce savings in the Navy's operating budget of $4 billion to $5 billion through fiscal 1980.[7] With no change in the current Navy plan to acquire twelve squadrons of F-14As, the reduction from twelve to nine carrier-attack air wings would produce investment savings totaling $7.5 billion through fiscal 1980. If it was decided not to proceed with the F-14B and to substitute improved RF-4s for the reconnaissance version of the F-14, annual investment costs for the Navy would be about $2.3 billion a year less by 1980 under this proposal.

Many analysts have questioned the practice of maintaining a one-to-one ratio of attack air wings to carrier decks, however, contending that, since not all of the carriers in commission are operational at any given time, not every ship requires a full air wing of its own. Their position has been strengthened by the decision to assign to the attack carriers the responsibility for ASW operations in addition to their former duties, an action that in effect increases the ratio of air wings to carrier decks to 4–3. The Navy is expected to maintain three ASW wings indefinitely, but the combined capacity of the carrier fleet will not be adequate to accommodate this force and the full complement of attack wings at the same time.[8]

7. This estimate excludes any savings that might be produced by corresponding reductions in the Navy's escort and replenishment ships, many of which are directly committed to supporting the aircraft carriers.

8. The twelve carriers projected for 1980 under the present course will have an aggregate capacity index of 1,644 (the total number of representative A-4 aircraft—

With the three ASW wings a force of nine attack wings would preserve the traditional one-to-one ratio of wings to ships and should therefore be adequate to support the twelve-carrier force the Navy plans. Similarly, with only nine ships in commission (as this option proposes), a force of six attack wings should suffice.

The Navy argues in contravention that it needs the operational flexibility provided by a surplus of aircraft over in-service carrier capacity. Retaining twelve attack wings for twelve carriers preserves the option of placing on every ship at sea a full complement of aircraft for attack operations while also allowing an additional reserve of aircraft (from the wings displaced from ships in overhaul) upon which to draw to replace combat losses.

Others find it difficult to envision a situation that would require every available ship for attack operations while posing no submarine threat to divert carrier capacity to ASW operations. They point out that the argument for extra aircraft to replace combat losses presumes that aircraft will be subject to attrition sooner than the carriers themselves, which is by no means clearly the case for all the contingencies in which carriers might be employed. Carriers could well be sunk or disabled under circumstances that would permit much of their aircraft complement to recover on other ships or on shore bases.

Accepting the argument that it is unnecessary to maintain one full attack wing for each carrier in commission (i.e., providing six rather than nine attack air wings for the nine-carrier force this option proposes[9]) would produce additional savings of $2.5 billion through 1980 and generate recurring annual savings of about $600 million thereafter.

Taken together, the actions affecting the Navy's tactical air forces proposed under this option would save an estimated $14 billion to $15 billion from fiscal 1975 to 1980. By the end of 1980 the force of nine carriers and six attack air wings would cost nearly $4 billion a year less to support and operate than the twelve carriers and twelve attack air wings projected under current policy. Attendant reductions in naval escort and auxiliary forces could generate additional annual savings of several hundred million dollars.

the smallest type operated by the Navy—that the ships could accommodate). However, the aggregate load index for the Navy's air wings will be at least 1,900 (about 1,640 for the twelve attack wings at their projected strength and composition plus 250 to 300 for the three ASW wings).

9. Under the present course the three wings assigned to Nimitz-class carriers would be expanded to include six squadrons each.

The necessity for the Marine Corps to continue to maintain three active air wings, each linked with a surface division to form one Marine amphibious force, has also been questioned. The close coordination between air and surface forces required for an amphibious assault is set forth to justify this special arrangement. As noted in chapter 5, however, the Navy does not have the means and the nation is not likely to have occasion to use all the available Marine forces this way.

The Marine Corps has no weapons acquisition programs under way comparable in scope to the largest Air Force and Navy programs but is nonetheless expected to invest an average of nearly $600 million a year to modernize its air wings from 1975 to 1980.[10] The largest amounts will be for acquiring a limited number of F-14s (four squadrons, or enough to modernize about one-quarter of present Marine Corps fighter strength) and for developing a replacement (the AV-16) for the recently introduced Harrier (AV-8) light attack squadrons. A one-wing reduction in Marine tactical air strength, together with a return to improved F-4s in place of F-14s for modernizing fighter squadrons[11] and a slowing of the AV-16 development program to match its pace to a service life for the AV-8 comparable to that expected for other fighter-attack aircraft,[12] would cut costs by over $4 billion through 1980 and produce recurring savings of over $1 billion a year into the 1980s.

These wings would be more than adequate to support all the surface forces that might be used in some future amphibious assault. Air reinforcements, should they become necessary, would be available from the Marine Reserve Air Wing and of course the Navy's carrier forces. Air support for the third active Marine division would become the responsibility of the Air Force—the service that would furnish the air support for the Army divisions alongside which the Marine division would be most likely to fight.

The cumulative effect of these actions—a smaller but fully modernized fourteen-wing Air Force specialized for battlefield operations, a Pacific-oriented fleet of nine carriers operating six attack and three ASW air

10. Marine Corps tactical air investment is funded in Navy research and development and procurement appropriations, as are non-personnel-related operating costs.

11. Navy arguments that Marine F-14s would be needed to help protect aircraft carriers supporting amphibious operations was a major factor in the decision by the Corps to participate in the F-14 program. But the Navy would have enough F-14s to protect the smaller carrier force proposed in this option without Marine assistance.

12. New fighter-attack designs are ordinarily expected to remain in service from twelve to fifteen years. The Marine Corps wants to replace the AV-8 after half this time.

Table 6-3. Projected Costs of Tactical Air Forces under Option C,
Reduced Force Levels, Fiscal Years 1975–80
Billions of fiscal 1975 dollars

| | | | | | | | 1975–80 | |
Type of cost	1975	1976	1977	1978	1979	1980	Total	Change^a
Investment	9.4	7.5	6.8	6.2	5.6	5.4	40.9	−16.8
Major systems	4.5	3.1	2.6	2.2	1.7	1.6	15.7	−14.7
Other	4.9	4.4	4.2	4.0	3.9	3.8	25.2	−2.1
Operations	13.3	12.6	11.8	11.1	10.6	10.6	70.0	−13.4
Active forces	5.7	5.2	4.7	4.1	3.7	3.7	27.1	−9.2
Reserve forces	1.2	1.3	1.4	1.5	1.5	1.7	8.6	+0.5
Indirect support	6.4	6.1	5.7	5.5	5.4	5.2	34.3	−4.7
Total	22.7	20.1	18.6	17.3	16.2	16.0	110.9	−30.2
Change^a	−0.9	−3.0	−4.0	−5.7	−8.0	−8.6	−30.2	...

Source: Author's estimates.
a. From projected present program.

wings, and a reduction of one Marine wing—would reduce the cost of the tactical air forces through 1980 by $30 billion. Annual costs would be reduced by $4 billion by 1977; by $8 billion to $9 billion by 1980.

The budget for the forces proposed in this option is presented in Table 6-3. The contribution of each proposal in lowering costs is shown in Table 6-4.

Option D: Greater Reliance on Air Power

The strongest proponents of air power argue that present policy errs in not fully exploiting the comparative advantage of the United States over its potential adversaries in technological assets; that the new tactical aircraft are proportionately no more expensive in relation to the designs they will replace than were the aircraft introduced ten or twenty years ago to their predecessors; and that the United States should devote more, not less, of its resources to tactical air power, financing the expansion if necessary by reductions in the less capital-intensive components of the general purpose forces.

The case for slowing the pace of modernization (Option A) centers on the general argument that technological progress in recent years has not achieved improvements in aircraft performance without incurring disproportionate increases in unit cost. While there is a theoretical foundation for this in the law of diminishing returns, there is no way to prove con-

Table 6-4. Budgetary Savings Resulting from Actions Proposed under Option C, Fiscal Years 1975–80
Billions of fiscal 1975 dollars

Service and proposed action	Savings, fiscal 1975–80			Annual savings by fiscal 1980		
	Investment	Operations	Total	Investment	Operations	Total
Air Force Eliminate Air Force deep penetration capability; retain buildup in close support capability as under current policy	5.6	6.1	11.7	2.0	1.7	3.7
Navy a. Limit sea-based air capability to Pacific; eliminate forces oriented toward NATO contingencies	7.5	4.4	11.9	2.3	0.9	3.2
b. Restore 1–1 ratio of air wings (attack plus antisubmarine) to carrier decks	1.0	1.5	2.5	0.2	0.4	0.6
Marine Corps Align Marine air strength to existing capability and likely requirements for amphibious assault; replace F-4 with improved F-4	2.7	1.4	4.1	0.7	0.4	1.1
Total	16.8	13.4	30.2	5.2	3.4	8.6

Source: Author's estimates.

clusively that an F-15 or an F-14 does not offer sufficient improvements in performance over existing F-4s to justify its greater costs any more than there is to prove the reverse. In view of this uncertainty, some contend that the benefit of the doubt should continue to be awarded to the new designs. Because U.S. general purpose forces are so heavily reliant on air power, it is argued, every effort should be made to minimize the risk that large numbers of U.S. aircraft might prove qualitatively inferior to those of the other side. Rather than further curtail the rate of modernization projected under present plans (estimated at under 5 percent a year), Option D would restore the pace of modernization to the average of 10 percent a year achieved during the 1960s.

Fundamental to the rationale underlying Options B and C is a rejection of the value in a conventional war of the deep penetration missions on which current USAF doctrine places such importance. In Option B the resources freed by deemphasizing the capability for such missions were reinvested, for the most part, to increase the Air Force's battlefield support capability. In Option C the savings were applied to reduce the defense budget. Option C realized further cost reductions by repudiating the Navy's position on the utility of large attack carriers against the sophisticated opposition that would be encountered in a European conflict and by balancing the Marine Corps's air support capability with the existing capability of the Navy to transport amphibious assault forces. Option D takes the opposite position on all these issues.

Full modernization of the Air Force's multipurpose fighter-bomber squadrons with the F-15 would be budgeted, as would efforts to continue developing refinements to this design. F-15s would be introduced as one-for-one replacements for F-4s, with the last F-4 squadrons converting to the F-15 in 1980. To achieve this schedule, the rate of procurement of the F-15 would double from the peak rate of 144 aircraft a year projected for the present program. Procuring the additional 730 F-15s required by 1980 under this option would cost $7.2 billion more than the $6.6 billion called for by the present program. An additional 240 F-15s, costing $2.3 billion, would be procured after 1980 to support the fourteen wings of F-15s throughout the design's expected service life. Unless present estimates of the cost of operating the F-15 prove unduly optimistic, the active Air Force operating budget should be little affected by this action. The large number of F-4s released from active duty would, as in Option C, be used to modernize the Air National Guard's F-100 squadrons, increasing the operating costs of these forces by about $100 million a year.

The Navy would receive enough F-14s to equip each of its carriers with two squadrons, replacing its entire F-4 inventory by 1980. Similarly, the Marine Corps would modernize its F-4 squadrons in the same period, procuring 320 additional F-14s at a cost of $4.8 billion. All would be the more powerful "B" models, but the aircraft procured for the Marine Corps would not be equipped with Phoenix missiles. As projected under the present course, a program to upgrade part of the F-14A force to the "B" design would be undertaken at the end of the decade. An additional $2.7 billion to procure the final 80 F-14s required to support full modernization of Navy and Marine fighter forces would be spent after the forecast period. There would be no change in Navy or Marine tactical air force levels from those currently planned.

Programs to modernize the reconnaissance arms of the services with RF-14s and RF-15s, expected to begin in the late 1970s under the current course, would be accelerated under this option at an additional cost of $1.8 billion.

Procurement of the A-10 would be increased to provide sufficient aircraft to equip and sustain a force of ten wings, half of them with A-10Bs carrying an all-weather avionics system. These wings would be introduced as additions to the existing force structure rather than as replacements for other types of aircraft. If one wing of F-111s was converted to electronic warfare, this would lead to a thirty-wing USAF fighter-attack strength by 1980—an increase of eight wings over the force projected for that year under current policy. Augmented as necessary by the existing force of A-7s, which would be maintained at the three-wing level, one wing of attack aircraft would be teamed with each Army division,[13] assuring the Army of at least as much battlefield air support by 1980 as the Marine Corps now gives its surface forces. The additional cost, including expansion of the AWACS program and increases in operational support in line with the increased combat force levels, is estimated at $4.2 billion for fiscal 1975–80. By 1980 annual operating costs would be about $1 billion a year more than is projected under present policy.

The lightweight fighter would not be needed under this option, which gives full responsibility for counterair operations to the large force of

13. Depending on what reductions in land forces accompanied the buildup in air power proposed in this option, fewer close air support wings might be required to achieve a ratio of one wing to one division. Alternatively, more than one close support wing could be teamed with each division. Another possibility would be smaller Army divisions, with the reduction in combat manpower compensated for by increased firepower provided through additional air support.

F-15s that is provided. Its development, as well as the follow-on air combat fighter program, would be promptly terminated, at an estimated saving in research and development costs of $200 million. Funding would be provided to support all other major weapons acquisition programs, including the AMST, AV-16, and Sparrow IIIF as well as the numerous older established systems, on the same scale as under the current course. In addition to the AMST the Air Force would undertake the development of a lighter vertical or short-takeoff-and-landing (V/STOL) transport for its airlift forces (designated TASTOL). To fund this effort, $0.8 billion is provided and the first squadrons would be formed by 1980.

Under this option capabilities in all mission areas would increase. The most substantial gains would be realized by the Air Force. For missions requiring a deep penetration capability, the Air Force would have 1,220 unit equipment aircraft by 1980 under both Option D and the current course, but better than 80 percent would have been modernized with the F-15 under this option and only about 35 percent under the current plan. Close support capability would increase well beyond what is projected under the present course. Instead of a unit equipment strength of 360 A-10s for battlefield attack, the Air Force would have 940 aircraft adept at this mission.

The air defenses of the Navy's attack carriers would be made as proficient as is technologically possible by full modernization with the F-14, although the present offensive capability of the carrier fleet, measured by the number of attack sorties it could launch, would not increase directly. Marine Corps ability to gain control of the air over contested beachheads would improve with full modernization of its fighter squadrons with the F-14.

Approximately 5,000 aircraft, including 3,600 fighter and attack types, would be procured from fiscal 1975 to 1980 to support this option, whereas fewer than 3,000 (2,100 fighter and attack types) are projected under current policy. Investment in acquiring major weapons systems during these six years would increase by over 60 percent, from $30.4 billion under current policy to about $50 billion. By 1980 the annual investment budget would be $6 billion higher and annual operating costs an estimated $1.2 billion higher under this option than under current policy.

The budget required to carry out this option is shown in Table 6-5.

Table 6-5. Projected Costs of Tactical Air Forces under Option D,
Greater Reliance on Air Power, Fiscal Years 1975–80
Billions of fiscal 1975 dollars

							1975–80	
Type of cost	*1975*	*1976*	*1977*	*1978*	*1979*	*1980*	*Total*	*Change*[a]
Investment	9.8	10.3	11.3	14.5	16.1	16.6	78.6	+20.9
Major systems	4.9	5.7	6.6	9.7	11.2	11.6	49.7	+19.3
Other	4.9	4.6	4.7	4.8	4.9	5.0	28.9	+1.6
Operations	13.7	13.9	14.1	14.2	14.5	15.2	85.6	+2.2
Active forces	6.0	6.1	6.2	6.2	6.3	6.6	37.4	+1.1
Reserve forces	1.2	1.3	1.3	1.4	1.5	1.7	8.4	+0.3
Indirect support	6.5	6.5	6.6	6.6	6.7	6.9	39.8	+0.8
Total	23.5	24.2	25.4	28.7	30.6	31.8	164.2	+23.1
Change[a]	−0.1	+1.1	+2.8	+5.7	+6.4	+7.2	+23.1	...

Source: Author's estimates.
a. From projected present program.

CHAPTER SEVEN

SUMMARY

Advancing technology has fostered a trend among all military powers toward greater reliance on weapons to wage war and less on direct human participation. In the language of economics, the military forces of the world, like its industries, have grown steadily more capital-intensive, substituting the firepower and mobility of war machines for battlefield manpower on an ever-increasing scale. With technology as the spur, it is not surprising that the United States, the nation with the richest technical endowment, should take the lead in this continuing process.

Although the singular difficulties one encounters in trying to measure military "output" make it impossible to demonstrate definitively that technological substitution has increased the economic efficiency of U.S. military forces, there can be little doubt that on the whole it has. Even if it had not, one might still argue that replacing combat manpower with combat machine power is worthwhile on the grounds that if wars must be fought it is better that they be fought as much with dollars and as little with lives as technology will permit. And there is strong evidence to suggest that the ascendancy of weapons over warriors, with its corollary that proportionately fewer U.S. soldiers need be exposed to the hazards of direct battle, has indeed substantially reduced the human cost of war to the United States by lowering the rate at which casualties are incurred.

Nonetheless, the exponentially climbing dollar cost of the progressively more sophisticated weapon systems that must be provided if the substitution process is to continue has raised concern to a crescendo. Without denying the advantages that have accrued from the man-to-machines trend in the past and keeping in mind that economic cost-effectiveness criteria alone are too narrow to appraise its full significance, one can still question its current pace. The apprehension of many seems to arise from the suspicion that too often in recent years new weapons have been introduced prematurely, before technological progress has accumulated enough innovations to give them the extra capability that would justify their extra cost. In some instances overall capability may actually diminish with a new system—because its performance, however promising on paper, falls below that of its more reliable predecessor in the field, because the constraint of total cost compels a replacement ratio so low it more than cancels any qualitative gains in unit performance, or simply because the new weapon's special capability is not the one most needed.

Outside the nuclear realm, the most pronounced manifestation of technological substitution within the armed forces has been the growth of tactical air power, components of which are to be found in all four services. For at least the past decade and probably as far back as World War II, tactical air forces have been the leading budgetary beneficiary in the general purpose forces of the emerging primacy of hardware over humans. Inasmuch as the Department of Defense budget submission for 1975 includes procurement funds for seven new (not yet fully operational) major weapon systems, development funding for six more systems with major program potential, and continued procurement spending on a dozen established systems, this distinction seems likely to be preserved throughout the 1970s.

Yet nowhere is the question of economic justification more pressing or the answer more elusive than it is for these systems and the missions they are designed to perform. Over the course of three decades, the real (adjusted to allow for inflation) cost of producing a single tactical fighter has, with remarkable consistency, doubled on average once every four years. The problem of how to continue to exploit the comparative advantage in technology this country enjoys in the face of unit costs that have risen to proportions which threaten to price many systems built to traditional U.S. standards out of the market is a serious and growing challenge for defense decision makers, military tacticians and weapons providers alike.

For the tactical air forces, meeting this challenge can only begin with a thorough reexamination of long-standing, cherished dogma concerning mission priorities, and the philosophy by which tactical aircraft are designed and built. Some changes in prevailing doctrine may be unavoidable as it becomes simply too expensive to buy in any substantial quantity aircraft with the performance characteristics needed to carry out the demanding missions the services consider vital. Current policy for the most part reflects both a reaffirmation of traditional service doctrines and values, tempered somewhat by concessions to the reality of rising unit costs, and the conviction that unilateral U.S. force reductions are unwise for the present.

About $140 billion[1] will be spent on Air Force, Navy, and Marine tactical air forces through 1980. This budget will sustain numerical strength near the current level but allow modernization at only half the rate realized during the 1960s (an average of less than 5 percent a year through 1980 as against the average of 10 percent in the 1960s). The long-range offensive capability of the Air Force will be preserved with the introduction of the F-15, and its close air support capability will be improved if proposals to introduce the A-10 overcome congressional opposition. Introducing the A-10 as a replacement for A-7 light attack aircraft, as the Air Force now plans to do, will have the least adverse effect on other mission capabilities—that is, short of adding the new A-10s to the force structure.

One measure of offensive striking power, aggregate lift capacity, has nearly doubled since 1960. By this standard, total capacity will not change appreciably during the rest of the 1970s. A slight reduction in the aggregate lift capacity of the active forces is forecast, but this will be offset by gains for the reserve components.

In the future, as in the past, most of the money for the tactical air forces will be spent on two exclusively American conventional war capabilities: deep penetration attack and sea-based tactical air operations. The feasibility of paying the great costs of continuing to maintain either or both of these capabilities on so large a scale is a central issue in the tactical air budget. The present course, as reflected in the 1975 budget, deals affirmatively with this issue on both points. Unwavering confidence in the utility of the Navy's large attack carriers is evidenced by the continued large-scale funding of F-14 procurement (as well as by last year's decision to proceed with construction of a fourth nuclear-powered carrier), while acquisition of the F-15 demonstrates a determination to maintain the Air Force's deep penetration capability. Confidence in a third capability, which no other nation possesses on the same scale as the United States, that of the Marines for amphibious assault, is also reaffirmed in the decisions to commence development of a new vertical or short-takeoff-and-landing support aircraft to replace the AV-8 Harrier and to provide the Corps with F-14s.

Although the present course would modernize the combat forces more slowly than in the 1960s, some observers believe that continued rampant

---

1. All cost estimates are expressed in dollars of constant fiscal 1975 purchasing power.

escalation in weapon system costs compels a still slower pace. Critics of the latest generation of high performance fighter-bombers, the Air Force F-15 Eagle and the Navy F-14 Tomcat, doubt that these aircraft offer sufficient improvements in performance over existing F-4 Phantom IIs to justify their much higher unit cost. Others accept the contention that the new designs will prove cost-effective but see no need for the capabilities that would be added if these aircraft replaced existing designs one-for-one, as is now planned.

One alternative would be to limit future modernization of the long-range multipurpose aircraft to improved models of the F-4. Without reducing force levels or curtailing the planned improvement in Air Force close support capability (through procurement of the A-10), this option could save $12 billion to $13 billion during the 1975–80 period, and reduce the annual tactical air budget by $3 billion by fiscal 1980 from the projected costs under current policy. Capabilities would be little affected in the near future by halting procurement of the F-14 and F-15; the long-term consequences would be largely dependent on what actions the Soviet Union took to modernize its forces. As a hedge against the possibility that it might quickly (though untypically) introduce large numbers of demonstrably superior aircraft, the United States could maintain a standby production potential for the F-15.

A more fundamental change calling for the restructuring of the Air Force to emphasize battlefield missions by replacing long-range multipurpose aircraft, both existing and planned, with new systems designed for close support and local air superiority would also produce savings in excess of $10 billion over the next six years and generate recurring annual savings of $3 billion to $4 billion thereafter. No reduction in the force levels or the overall pace of modernization projected under the present course would be required. Slower modernization of the Navy and the Marine Corps would be more than offset by faster modernization of the Air Force.

Reequipping existing Air Force multipurpose fighter-bomber squadrons with specialized lightweight fighters and A-10 close support aircraft would mean giving up the present ability to mount a massive conventional air interdiction campaign and with it the doctrine of total air supremacy. Advocates of this course argue that in the principal contingency for which the United States prepares, an attack on NATO in Europe, the conventional phase would almost certainly be brief and that existing doctrine is ill suited and existing forces ill configured to fight a

Table 7-1. Current and Alternative Tactical Air Programs

Characteristic	Projected present course	Option A, slower modernization	Option B, reordered mission priorities	Option C, reduced force levels	Option D, greater reliance on air power
Force levels, fiscal 1980 (number of fighter-attack wings)					
Air Force	22	22	22	14	30
Navy	12	12	12	6	12
Marine Corps	3	3	3	2	3
Force structure by mission capability, fiscal 1980 (number of unit equipment aircraft)					
Deep penetration, total	**2,340**	**2,340**	**1,550**	**900**	**2,320**
Air Force	1,220	1,220	430	290	1,220
Navy	760	760	760	400	760
Marine Corps	360	360	360	210	340
Battlefield operations, total[a]	**470**	**470**	**1,260**	**800**	**1,050**
Air Force	360	360	1,150	720	940
Navy	0	0	0	0	0
Marine Corps	110	110	110	80	110
Average annual modernization rate, fiscal 1975–80[b]	**4.7**	**2.2**	**4.9**	**7.1**	**10.4**
Cost (billions of fiscal 1975 dollars)					
Total, fiscal 1975–80	**141**	**129**	**129**	**111**	**164**
Investment	58	46	47	41	79
Operations	83	83	82	70	86

Source: Author's estimates.

a. Includes local counterair lightweight fighters and attack aircraft specialized for close support (AV-8, AV-16, AH-1, and A-10). Existing light attack designs (A-4 and A-7) are included in the deep penetration category.

b. Average annual percentage of fighter-attack squadrons reequipped with aircraft of new design series. Does not include "in series" modernization, such as the provision of the improved F-4.

short, intense conflict. The goal of total victory in the air before all else may well be unrealistically ambitious against the Warsaw Pact countries, and unnecessary except as a precondition to interdiction. However successful, such an effort would be quite costly in allied aircraft and aircrews and to achieve significant results would require months, at best. Diverting resources to airbase attack and deep interdiction at the expense of close air support for land forces on the battlefield, the effect of which would be felt immediately, could well prove a decisive error in a short war. Reordering mission priorities would not only lower defense costs but might well lead to a more formidable defensive posture in Europe.

Alternatively, the savings that would ensue from deemphasizing deep penetration missions could be applied in full to reduce the defense budget, rather than being reinvested in further improving battlefield support capability. The reduced force levels that this deemphasis would make possible, coupled with a more realistic view of the value of aircraft carriers in the European theater and with a reduction in Marine Corps air strength to a level in balance with its amphibious assault capability, would save $30 billion through 1980 and lower the annual budget by $8 billion to $9 billion in the years following.

Taking the opposite tack, others believe that the air arm of the general purpose forces offers untapped opportunities for the United States to exploit its technical advantage over other nations, and that more, not fewer, resources ought to be devoted to tactical air power. While few would argue that the substitution of technology for combat manpower can be pursued to the point of abolishing use of the latter at any time in the foreseeable future, past benefits from this process, the foremost of which may be lower military casualties, might be cited as reasons for continuing the substitution process. A fourth option, which would preserve the pace of modernization at about the rate of the 1960s, increasing close support capability well above that projected under the present program while providing for fully modernized deep penetration, carrier air defense, and Marine counterair forces, would raise tactical air costs by about $25 billion over the next six years. The larger forces proposed under this option would cost about $8 billion more a year to operate and sustain during the 1980s than the forces projected to evolve under current policy.

The salient features of each of these options are compared with the projected present course in Table 7-1; additional information about force levels and procurement requirements is given in Appendix A.

Each reader's choice, then, will depend on his or her assessment of the arguments pro and con; and this in turn will be shaped by perceptions of the international political scene, the likelihood of conflict, and the form it might take. This study has attempted to indicate some of the quantitative implications of that choice, in force levels and defense spending, and to stress the urgency of making it. The United States stands on the verge of commitments to tactical air programs that, once made, will be difficult to reverse and whose implications will play a large part in shaping its military capabilities and the defense budget through the 1980s. These commitments should not be made without a clear understanding of these implications and of available alternatives. If this paper provides a solid basis for that understanding, it will have served its purpose.

Projections of Force Levels, Aircraft Procurement, and Costs

Table A-1. Projected Tactical Air Force Structure under Present Policy, Fiscal Years 1974–80

Service, mission, and type of aircraft	Unit equipment aircraft per squadron	Number of squadrons at end of year						
		1974	*1975*	*1976*	*1977*	*1978*	*1979*	*1980*
Air Force		**122**	**123**	**120**	**116**	**116**	**117**	**117**
Fighter and attack								
F-4	18 or 24	43	43	40	37	30	27	24
F-111	24	12	12	12	11	10	9	9
F-15	24	0	1	3	6	12	15	18
A-7	24	9	9	9	6	6	3	...
A-10(A)[a]	24	0	0	0	3	6	12	15
Subtotal		64	65	64	63	64	66	66
Reconnaissance and electronic warfare								
EB-66	12	1	1	1	1	...	...	...
RF-4	18	13	13	13	12	12	11	9
RF-15	18	0	0	0	0	0	1	3
F-4	18	2	2	2	3	4	4	4
F-105	18	2	2	2	1	...	...	...
EF-111	18	0	0	0	0	1	2	3
Subtotal	...	18	18	18	17	17	18	19
Airlift								
C-130	16	17	17	16	15	15	14	12
AMST	16	0	0	0	0	0	1	3
Subtotal		17	17	16	15	15	15	15
Special operating forces[b]	Varied	6	6	5	4	3	...	...
Tactical operations[c]	Varied	17	17	17	17	17	18	18
Navy		**104**	**106**	**107**	**108**	**104**	**99**	**99**
Fighter and attack								
F-8	12	4	4	2	2	...	...	...
F-4	12	20	19	18	16	15	12	12
F-14	12	4	6	8	10	11	12	12
A-4	14	3	3	3	3	...	...	...
A-6	12	12	12	12	12	12	12	12
A-7	12	27	27	28	28	28	27	27
Subtotal		70	71	71	71	66	63	63

Table A-1 (*continued*)

Service, mission, and type of aircraft	Unit equipment aircraft per squadron	Number of squadrons at end of year						
		1974	1975	1976	1977	1978	1979	1980
Reconnaissance and electronic warfare[d]								
EA-6	4	6	7	9	11	12	12	12
RF-8	3	5	5	4	3	2	1	...
RA-5	4	9	9	9	9	9	7	6
RF-14	4	0	0	0	0	2	4	6
Subtotal		20	21	22	23	25	24	24
Tactical operations[e]	Varied	14	14	14	14	13	12	12
Marine Corps		**61**	**61**	**62**	**63**	**63**	**63**	**63**
Fighter and attack								
F-4	15	12	11	10	9	8	8	8
F-14	12	0	1	2	3	4	4	4
A-4	16 or 20	5	5	5	6	6	6	6
A-6	12	5	5	6	6	6	6	6
AV-8	20	3	3	3	3	3	3	2
AV-16	20	0	0	0	0	0	0	1
AH-1	18	3	3	3	3	3	3	3
Subtotal		28	28	29	30	30	30	30
Reconnaissance and electronic warfare								
RF-4	9	3	3	3	3	3	3	3
EA-6	7	3	3	3	3	3	3	3
Subtotal		6	6	6	6	6	6	6
Airlift[f]	18, 21, or 24	21	21	21	21	21	21	21
Tactical operations[g]	18	6	6	6	6	6	6	6

Source: Author's estimates.

a. Fair weather version only. The analysis assumes that three wings of A-10s replace A-7s on a one-for-one basis, one wing of A-10s replaces one wing of F-111s converted to an electronic warfare mission capability, and a fifth wing of A-10s is added to the force structure.

b. Includes AC-119s, AC-130s, B-57s, and miscellaneous types.

c. Includes OV-10s, EC-121s, EC-135s, and miscellaneous types.

d. Organized in detachments.

e. Includes E-1s, E-2s, UH-2s, SH-3s, and miscellaneous types.

f. Includes UH-1, CH-46, and CH-53 helicopter troop carriers.

g. Includes OV-10 light armed reconnaissance aircraft and miscellaneous types.

Table A-2. Comparison of Active Fighter and Attack Force Levels under Alternative Programs, Fiscal Years 1974 and 1980

Number of unit equipment aircraft

Service and type of aircraft	Fiscal 1974	Fiscal 1980				
		Present program	Option A, slower modern- ization	Option B, reordered mission priorities	Option C, reduced force levels	Option D, greater reliance on air power
Air Force						
F-4	936	576	960	96	...	...
F-111	288	216	216	144	144	216
F-15	...	432	48	48	144	1,008
LWF	...	...	...	648	360	...
A-7	216	...	...	144	...	216
A-10	...	360	360	504	360	360
A-10B	...	...	...	...	...	360
Subtotal	1,440	1,584	1,584	1,584	1,008	2,160
Navy						
F-8	48	...	...	...	...	...
F-4	240	144	192	192	...	...
F-14	48	144	96	96	144	288
A-4	42	...	...	...	...	...
A-6	144	144	144	144	72	144
A-7	324	324	324	324	180	324
Subtotal	846	756	756	756	396	756
Marine Corps						
F-4	180	120	180	180	90	...
F-14	...	48	...	...	...	144
A-4	80	120	120	120	80	120
A-6	60	72	72	72	48	72
AV-8A	60	40	60	60	40	40
AV-16	...	20	...	...	...	20
AH-1	54	54	54	54	36	54
Subtotal	434	474	486	486	294	450
Total	2,720	2,814	2,826	2,826	1,698	3,366

Source: Author's estimates.

Table A-3. Comparison of Tactical Aircraft Procurement under Alternative Programs, Fiscal Years 1975-80

Number of aircraft

Mission and type of aircraft	Projected present course	Option A, slower modern- ization	Option B, reordered mission priorities	Option C, reduced force levels	Option D, greater reliance on air power
Fighter and attack					
F-14A	150	...	...	90	150
F-14B	80[a]	[b]	...	...	320
F-15	565	...	...	160	1,300
F-4	...	600	200	120	...
LWF	...	...	1,200	730	...
A-10A	729	729	950	730	730
A-10B[c]	...	...	...	...	650
AV-16	40[a]	...	...	...	40
Other[d]	450	450	450	80	450
Subtotal	2,110	1,780	2,800	1,910	3,640
Combat support					
EF-111	70	70	...	...	70
RF-14	60[a]	...	...	...	130
RF-15	70[a]	...	...	...	150
RF-4	...	120	120	50	...
AMST	180[a]	...	...	...	180
TASTOL[e]	...	...	70	...	70
Other	60	100	200	60	200
Subtotal	440	290	390	110	800
All other	400	400	400	200	600
Total	2,950	2,470	3,590	2,220	5,040

Source: Author's estimates.
a. Assumed initiatives (no formal procurement program yet announced).
b. Continuing research and development on engines.
c. With all-weather avionics.
d. Excludes aircraft procured solely for U.S. allies.
e. Smaller vertical or short-takeoff-and-landing (V/STOL) airlifter proposed as alternative to advanced medium short-takeoff-and-landing transport (AMST).

NATO and the Warsaw Pact: The Balance in the Air

Various unclassified sources place the operational strength of the Soviet Union's tactical air force at between 4,000 and 5,000 aircraft. If the midpoint in this estimate is taken as correct and reconnaissance types, of which there are probably at least 500, are excluded, Soviet strength in combat aircraft is about 4,000. Forty percent of this force is equipped with modern strike aircraft, mostly SU-7 Fitters and YAK-28 Brewers, which have a significant capability for attacking surface targets at short range.[1] Another 1,200–1,400 older, now obsolescent MIG-17s, MIG-19s, and IL-28s might also be used to provide air support on the battlefield, though their capability would be limited in this regard—the MIGs by their quite small payloads, the IL-28 by its vulnerability. It is believed that these types are being gradually phased out of the Soviet inventory and being replaced by the variable geometry MIG-23 Flogger, several hundred of which may already be in service.

Except for the IL-28, all these strike aircraft could also employ the cannons and rockets they carry in aerial combat, but in most cases their proficiency in a counterair role would be less than first rate. For this mission, the Russians rely on about 1,200 missile-armed MIGs, primarily various models of the MIG-21 Fishbed series although a few of the older MIG-17s and -19s may remain operational in this role. To reinforce these tactical counterair forces, the Soviet Union could draw on the nearly 3,000 interceptors that are assigned to strategic air defense, guarding the Soviet heartland against the nuclear threat posed by U.S., British, French, and Chinese manned bombers. About one-third of this force, or 1,000 aircraft, is equipped with the aging MIG-17s and -19s. Less readily spared from the strategic defenses are an estimated 800 SU-9 Fishpots, and

---

1. However, they carry much smaller payloads and are less accurate than the strike aircraft in the U.S. arsenal.

1,000–1,200 heavier twin-engine types: YAK-28s, the similar but less capable YAK-25s, and modern SU-11s and long-range TU-28s. New high-speed, high-altitude MIG-25s are believed to be joining the USSR's strategic defensive forces and perhaps the reconnaissance arm of its tactical forces as well.[2]

Other, nonnuclear members of the Warsaw Pact could contribute a total of 1,500 fighters to the air battle, half of which would be MIG-21s and half MIG-17s and -19s, if they retained none of their forces for strategic air defense. They also have about 500 strike aircraft, only about one-fourth of which are modern (SU-7s), however, the remainder being MIG-17s and IL-28s. All the combat aircraft of the Eastern European nations are of Soviet design.

The European members of NATO combined have about 1,900 aircraft (exclusive of reconnaissance types) assigned to tactical missions. Just under 800 of these aircraft are fighters with the primary mission of engaging the other side's tactical air forces; 1,100 have been assigned an attack role. Many of these also have a counterair capability and in fact, because of range and payload limitations, might prove more useful in this role than for strike missions. Most of the 600-plus interceptors assigned to strategic defense would also be potentially useful in the tactical air battle. In addition, Canada has 160 combat aircraft, about one-third of which are interceptors assigned to the North American Air Defense Command (NORAD).

The air assets of the European NATO countries are composed of a heterogeneous mix of nearly two dozen different designs, both U.S. and European. At present, the most numerous aircraft in these countries' arsenal are U.S.-designed F-104 Starfighters, a plane roughly comparable in performance to the Warsaw Pact countries' MIG-21. About 600 F-104s are with operating squadrons. Though a few have been assigned an attack role, use of most of these aircraft would be limited to air combat at short ranges. Several members of NATO have been replacing their F-104s, some (most notably, West Germany) with the F-4, which has much greater offensive capabilities. Another 300 aircraft in the European NATO inventory are F-5s, also specialized for close-in aerial combat.

The tactical air assets of the United States were discussed at length in

2. To be effective in a tactical combat role against high-performance fighters the MIG-25 would have to be equipped with an air-to-air missile system far superior to any now in existence in the West, including the U.S. Navy's Phoenix. The Soviet Union is not known to have such a system.

chapter 3, and a summary of unit equipment strength by service and kinds of aircraft for the active forces appears in the first column of Table A-2. In addition to the 2,800 tactical fighter and attack aircraft in the active forces (1,400 of which are F-4s), the reserves have another 1,000, half of which are F-100s, now suitable primarily for strike operations, but also retaining an air combat capability at least equal to that of the MIG-17s and -19s, SU-7s, and YAK-25s of the Warsaw Pact countries. The United States also has about 500 air defense interceptors, mostly in the Air National Guard, which theoretically might be committed to tactical counter-air operations.

The operational strength[3] of each side, including strategic defensive as well as tactical fighter-attack forces, is summarized in Table B-1. In simple numerical terms the two alliances are very nearly equal in tactical strength: 6,000 warplanes for the Warsaw Pact, 5,700 for NATO. The 5–2 superiority of the Soviet Union in interceptor aircraft over the combined assets of NATO, however, gives the Pact members an overall superiority of about 2,000 aircraft in the theoretical maximum strength that each side could commit to a major European war (8,900 versus 6,900).

Whereas the Pact countries have a modest overall numerical advantage, consideration of qualitative differences in the kinds of aircraft possessed by each side suggests that NATO has a clear advantage in terms of offensive capacity. Because the aircraft in the NATO, and especially the U.S., arsenal are on the average larger and able to carry heavier payloads over longer ranges than the aircraft of the Soviet Union and its allies, the aggregate lift capacity of the NATO side is half again as great as that of the Warsaw Pact.[4] The designs in use by the two alliances are shown in Table B-2.

While Table B-1 indicates the maximum forces that *could* be committed by each side, it would be unrealistic to anticipate that all these forces *would* be committed in the event. The table is the point of departure for a balance-of-force analysis, the latest set of "knowable" quantities, not the point of culmination. Each side labors under circumstances and priorities that would constrain both its willingness and its ability to bring

---

3. This is the estimated number of aircraft authorized for the operating forces, the figure probably most indicative of effective strength. Each side has a greater total number of aircraft than is shown in Table B-1, but not all of these are operationally available at any given time.

4. See page 17 for comments on the usefulness and limitations of this measure as a gross indicator of offensive capacity.

Table B-1. Tactical and Strategic Defense Air Assets of NATO and Warsaw Pact Members, by Number of Aircraft Assigned to Operating Squadrons and Designated Mission, Fiscal Year 1974

Alliance and member	Tactical fighter and attack			Strategic defense interceptors	Total combat strength[a]	Aggregate lift capacity (millions of pounds)
	Counterair	Strike	Total			
NATO						
United States	1,620	2,110	3,730	510	4,240	99
Active	1,480	1,250	2,730	130	2,860	76
Reserve	140	860	1,000	380	1,380	23
Allies	830	1,130	1,960	680	2,640	50
Total	2,450	3,240	5,690	1,190	6,880	149
Warsaw Pact						
USSR	1,200	2,800	4,000	2,900	6,900	80–90
Allies	1,500	500	2,000	...	2,000	14–16
Total	2,700	3,300	6,000	2,900	8,900	94–106

Sources: International Institute for Strategic Studies, *The Military Balance, 1973–1974* (London: IISS, 1973); *Jane's All the World's Aircraft* (London: Jane's Yearbooks, various years); T. N. Dupuy and Wendell Blanchard, *The Almanac of World Military Power,* 2d ed. (T. N. Dupuy Associates and R. R. Bowker Co., 1972).

a. Combat aircraft only; does not include reconnaissance, electronic warfare, airlift, or support aircraft.

all these assets to bear along a single line of confrontation. To progress further, certain assumptions must be made.

The first set of questions to be addressed is political. Which of the smaller nations might choose not to participate, fully or at all, in a war that might be construed as essentially a great-power struggle? And how much of the total resources available to the great powers, each of which has commitments and faces threats in other parts of the world, would they concentrate in the European theater?

Many analysts have come to doubt the reliability of several of the USSR's Eastern European allies, some to the point of questioning whether nations such as Hungary, Czechoslovakia, and the Balkan states, which at times have shown pronounced nationalistic proclivities, might not serve more to drain than to augment Soviet military resources in time of war. For NATO the chief question about participation pertains to France, which has pursued an increasingly independent policy on military matters in recent years.[5] These questions cannot be resolved here; rather it is as-

5. Despite the withdrawal of its forces from the NATO command structure, most analysts doubt that France could remain uninvolved in the event of a communist attack on West Germany. As this is being written the status of Greece, which is important to the defense of NATO's southern flank, is uncertain.

Table B-2. Designs in Use by NATO and Warsaw Pact Members, by Designated Mission

Alliance and member	Tactical fighter and attack		Strategic defense interceptors
	Counterair	Strike	
NATO			
U.S. active	F-4	A-4	F-106
	F-8	A-6	
		A-7	
		AH-1	
		AV-8	
		F-111	
U.S. reserve	F-4	F-100	F-101
	F-104	F-105	F-102
			F-106
Allies	Draken	AV-8	CF-101
	F-4	B-57	F-4
	F-5	Buccaneer	F-5
	F-86	F-5	F-86
	F-104	F-84F	F-102
	Mirage III	F-100	F-104
		F-104	Lightning
		G-91	Mirage III
		Hunter	Mystère IV
		Mirage III	Vantour II
		Mirage V	
		Super Mystère	
		Vantour II	
Warsaw Pact			
Soviet Union	MIG-17	IL-28	MIG-17
	MIG-19	MIG-17	MIG-19
	MIG-21	SU-7	MIG-25
	MIG-23	YAK-25	SU-9
		YAK-28	SU-11
			TU-28
			YAK-25
			YAK-28
Allies[a]	MIG-17	IL-28	
	MIG-19	MIG-17	
	MIG-21	SU-7	

Sources: Same as Table B-1.

a. Aircraft considered to be with the tactical counterair forces might be used as air defense interceptors if NATO threatened strategic attack.

sumed that each alliance would receive the unqualified support of all its member nations. This leaves the question of how much force the Soviet Union and the United States would be likely to hold back to meet contingencies in other parts of the world.

At present the Soviet Union is believed to have as much as one-third of its tactical air assets oriented toward the East, supporting the forty to fifty divisions positioned along its disputed border with the Peoples Republic of China. It seems plausible to assume that an essential precondition to any attack by the Warsaw Pact countries on Western Europe would be the achievement of some sort of understanding between the Soviet Union and Communist China that would free at least part of the military forces the USSR has pointed in this direction. It is unlikely, however, that Sino-Soviet relations will improve in the near future to the point where the USSR is willing to denude this theater entirely. A residual force of 500 aircraft might seem a reasonable Soviet hedge against the need for a holding action in the East.

It is equally unlikely that the United States would withdraw all of its forces in Asia or commit to the last squadron all of the tactical air forces based in the continental United States to meet even a worst-case conventional attack on NATO. A reasonable minimum presence in Asia might be two Air Force wings (one with squadrons positioned in Korea and Thailand, a second with squadrons in ready reserve on Okinawa and the Philippines), two attack carriers, and a Marine air wing. This reduction would free one wing of F-4s and one Navy carrier for transfer to Europe as reinforcements for the seven tactical fighter wings (six of F-4s, one of F-111s) deployed there and the two Navy carriers on station in the Mediterranean. Further reinforcements from active forces based in the United States might go as high as seven Air Force wings (leaving four) and two carriers from the Atlantic fleet. At most, two Marine air wings might also be sent to Europe.

A likely disposition for the thirty tactical fighter groups (equivalent to ten wings) in the Air National Guard and the Air Force Reserve, all of which are maintained in a high state of readiness, would be to deploy the equivalent of seven wings to Europe, holding three in the United States as stand-ins for the units in Europe. Marine and Navy reserves could be assumed to be held in the United States.

Table B-3 illustrates how U.S. tactical air forces might be redeployed to meet an all-out conventional attack by the Warsaw Pact countries. It is estimated that such redeployments could be essentially completed within thirty days under a maximum effort.

Finally, there is the question how heavily the two alliances might draw on their strategic defensive forces to bolster their strength for the tactical air battle. This issue is particularly significant for the Soviet Union, which maintains by far the largest force of air defense interceptors (see Table

Table B-3. Redisposition of U.S. Tactical Air Forces for NATO Defense

Service	Europe		Asia		United States	
	Wings	*Aircraft*	*Wings*	*Aircraft*	*Wings*	*Aircraft*
Peacetime disposition						
Air Force						
Active	7	500	3	220	11	790
Reserve	...	...	...	...	10	740
Navy						
Active	2	120	3	180	9	520
Reserve	...	...	...	...	2	110
Marine Corps						
Active	...	...	1	130	2	260
Reserve	...	...	...	...	1	160
Total	9	620	7	530	35	2,580
Disposition for NATO defense						
Air Force						
Active	15	1,090	2	140	4	280
Reserve	7	520	...	...	3	220
Navy						
Active	5	300	2	120	7	400
Reserve	...	...	...	...	2	110
Marine Corps						
Active	2	260	1	130	...	...
Reserve	...	...	...	...	1	160
Total	29	2,170	5	390	17	1,170

Source: Author's estimates.

B-1). The USSR faces a strategic threat from NATO of 540 manned bombers: 440 B-52s and FB-111s from the United States, 60 Vulcan bombers from the United Kingdom, and 40 French Mirage IVs. The People's Republic of China has as many as 100 TU-16 medium bombers, which could also deliver nuclear weapons against the Soviet Union's Asian republics (or the European heartland if committed to one-way missions by the Chinese), and probably enough nuclear warheads to equip this force. If the Chinese and the NATO strategic threats are taken together, the USSR maintains a ratio of about 4.5 interceptors for each bomber arrayed against it.

By comparison, NORAD, with a force of 550 interceptors (50 of them Canadian) protecting North America against a Soviet force of 140 long-range bombers and another 50 medium bombers that could reach NORAD targets with in-flight refueling, maintains only about 2.9 interceptors against each threatening bomber. The USSR has 650 additional medium bombers that could strike Great Britain and France, which together have only 260 interceptors facing this threat, or one interceptor for each 2.5 bombers. Both nations, however, would be at least partially shielded from nuclear attack by NATO's tactical counterair forces.

One can only guess how these interceptor forces might be reapportioned in the face of an intense conventional conflict. Certainly, the Soviet Union would transfer some interceptors to augment its tactical strength. It is much less likely that the United States, whose interceptor strength is not only much smaller in relation to the threat than that of the USSR but is also composed of aging models designed for destroying cumbersome bombers rather than sparring with agile fighters, would assign any of its strategic defensive forces to a tactical role. And Britain and France would almost certainly hold back all of their sparse interceptor forces. For the other members of NATO, which have no strategic nuclear forces and would therefore presumably be lower on the USSR's targeting list, commitment of air defense forces to the tactical battle might come more easily.

A reasonable course for the USSR to follow would be to reassign its MIG-17 and MIG-19 interceptors to tactical missions, retaining its newer, longer-ranged, and more capable designs to meet the manned bomber threat. Such a move would still leave nearly 2,000 interceptors to contend with the 540 NATO and 100 Chinese bombers that could strike Soviet targets, about the same 3–1 ratio as that NORAD maintains against the Soviet bomber threat. Of course, the long-range F-4 and F-111 fighter-bombers of the United States would also pose a strategic nuclear threat to the Soviet Union (see chapter 5) when deployed to European bases, and the USSR might hold additional interceptors in reserve to contend with this possibility. On the other hand, it could be argued that the best way for the USSR to defend itself against this threat (short of preemptive nuclear strikes against the fighter-bomber bases) would be to engage and reduce the U.S. F-4 and F-111 force early in the conventional tactical arena, in which case it might commit a larger portion of its air defense interceptors than the 1,000 assumed here.

Table B-4 shows the numerical strength of each side at the outset of a conventional war under the five assumptions discussed above, which can be summarized briefly.

First, all the member states within each alliance participate fully in the common war effort.

Table B-4. Tactical Air Strength of NATO and Warsaw Pact Members at Start of Conventional War

Alliance and member	Number of combat aircraft	Aggregate lift capacity (millions of pounds)
NATO		
United States	2,150	53
Based in Europe	650	18
Prompt reinforcements	1,500	35
Allies	2,350	44
Total	4,500	97
Warsaw Pact		
USSR	4,500	40–45
Allies	2,000	14–16
Total	6,500	54–61

Source: Author's estimates.

Second, U.S. reserve forces are promptly and effectively mobilized. The United States retains two tactical fighter wings (TFW), two air carrier wings (CVW), and one Marine air wing (MAW) positioned in Asia (about 10 percent of total operational strength), and the equivalent of seven TFWs, nine CVWs, and one MAW in reserve in the United States (30 percent of total operational strength).[6]

Third, the Soviet Union holds 500 tactical warplanes (12 percent of its total tactical operating strength) in Asia against contingencies on the Sino-Soviet border.

Fourth, interceptor forces (U.S. and Canadian) assigned to NORAD and those of the other nuclear-armed NATO members, Great Britain and France, are not committed to the conventional battle. All the interceptor forces of the other NATO members are committed.

Finally, the Soviet Union transfers 1,000 interceptors, about one-third of its strategic air defense force, to its tactical air force. The 1,900 interceptors held back for strategic air defense give the USSR about the same ratio (3–1) of interceptors to threatening bombers (including Chinese) as NORAD maintains. The other members of the Warsaw Pact use all their fighter-interceptors in a tactical counterair role.

6. If the situation deteriorated in Europe, with no outbreak of hostilities in Asia, the United States could commit additional forces from this reserve to Europe. Over half of the aircraft assumed to be held in this country belong to the Navy and the Marine Corps, however, perhaps limiting opportunities for their being used effectively in the European theater.

Not included in the totals shown in Table B-4 are the U.S. Army's helicopter gunships, several hundred of which could be used for close support duties. The Army believes this kind of weapon system to be highly effective in countering enemy armor. However, there is appreciable doubt about the survivability of helicopters over a battlefield that has the sophisticated antiair weapons available to the Warsaw Pact countries.

Under the foregoing assumptions NATO could expect to face a force numerically superior in combat aircraft by 50 percent. However, if the Soviet Union, for whatever reason—bureaucratic impediments (Soviet air defense forces enjoy greater status and organizational independence than similar elements in NATO) or the quasi-strategic threat of NATO fighter-bombers, for example—did not bolster its tactical strength with reinforcements from its air defense forces or felt it necessary to maintain greater strength along its Asian frontiers, the Warsaw Pact countries' numerical advantage over NATO could dwindle to approximate parity.

Even if none of these difficulties arose to prevent Warsaw Pact members from achieving the strength associated with a maximum effort, the comparatively lightweight, short-range character of Soviet-designed tactical aircraft, indicated by the "lift capacity" statistic, would still give NATO an advantage in offensive capacity by about the same 3–2 margin the Pact would enjoy in numbers. Other qualitative considerations, such as better-trained aircrews and a superior maintenance and logistical support infrastructure, also favor the NATO side.

On balance, NATO's qualitative advantages appear to more than outweigh its inferiority in number of aircraft. While NATO may have the stronger tactical air forces overall, it seems equally clear that the Warsaw Pact countries have a formidable capability as well, especially for counterair operations. The danger is that the Pact members' air strength might, in cooperation with the extensive antiair weapons in the hands of their ground forces, suffice to neutralize the advantage of NATO's air forces in offensive capacity. Certainly NATO's present superiority in the air is not so overwhelming that it can be relied upon to redress any serious imbalance that might develop between opposing surface forces.

U.S. Tactical Air Power
Missions, Forces, and Costs
WILLIAM D. WHITE

The cost of military weapons, particularly of warplanes, has risen at a startling rate since the Second World War. Although some of the increase can be attributed to inflation, most of it is due to the increasing sophistication of weapons. The steady incorporation of advancing technology in new weapon systems has been in part an outgrowth of the practice of replacing military personnel with military machines.

The author of this paper—the seventh in the Studies in Defense Policy series—contends that innovation has led to aircraft systems so large and complex, often without correspondingly improved performance and mission capability, that their cost threatens to become prohibitive. Moreover, the tactical missions that prevailing U.S. doctrine regards as most important—and that lead to complex and costly aircraft—may not be those that would prove most useful in honoring the nation's military commitments.

Present policy governing tactical air power, as reflected in the federal budget, continues to regard such missions as necessary and feasible and to judge their attendant costs acceptable. The author suggests four alternatives to the present course—a slower pace of modernization, reordered mission priorities, reduced force levels, and increased reliance on air power as a substitute for ground forces—and discusses how force structure, new aircraft, costs, and mission capabilities would vary with each alternative.

William D. White wrote this paper as a research associate in the Brookings Foreign Policy Studies program.

★ ★

BROOKINGS STUDIES IN DEFENSE POLICY

set forth the results of disinterested professional analysis of defense postures, policies, and budgets. Based solely upon unclassified and publicly available information, their purpose is to contribute to informed public debate on current and emerging defense issues.

★ ★

THE BROOKINGS INSTITUTION, WASHINGTON, D.C.

ISBN 0-8157-9371-5

Cover design: McIver Art